T0328407

GARLAND STUDIES ON

INDUSTRIAL
PRODUCTIVITY

edited by

STUART BRUCHEY
ALLAN NEVINS PROFESSOR EMERITUS
COLUMBIA UNIVERSITY

MANAGING THE BUSINESS

How Successful Managers Align Management Systems with Business Strategy

GARRY LEWIS McDANIEL

Routledge
Taylor & Francis Group

LONDON AND NEW YORK

First published 1999 by Garland Publishing Inc.

Published 2020 by Routledge
2 Park Square, Milton Park, Abingdon, Oxon, OX14 4RN
605 Third Avenue, New York, NY 10017

First issued in paperback 2021

Routledge is an imprint of the Taylor & Francis Group, an informa business

Publisher's Note
The publisher has gone to great lengths to ensure the quality of this reprint but points out that some imperfections in the original copies may be apparent.

Library of Congress Cataloging-in-Publication Data
McDaniel, Garry L.
    Managing the business : how successful managers align management systems with business strategy / Garry Lewis McDaniel.
        p. cm. — (Garland studies on industrial productivity)
    Includes bibliographical references and index.
    ISBN 0-8153-3691-8 (alk. paper)
    1. Management. 2. System theory. 3. Industrial productivity. I. Title.
II. Series.
HD31.M1545 1999
658.4 21—dc21   99-044758

ISBN 13: 978-1-138-98035-8 (pbk)
ISBN 13: 978-0-8153-3691-4 (hbk)
ISBN 13: 978-0-203-82353-8 (ebk)

DOI: 10.4324/9780203823538

Dedication

To Lauren, Ian and Julia . . .
you are my inspiration and guiding light.

Table of Contents

List of Tables

List of Figures

Preface

In today's fast-paced, dynamic and highly competitive work environment, organizations strive to attract and develop strong leaders and managers. Not surprisingly, organizations are also interested in determining what qualities or characteristics the best leaders and managers exhibit, and how to develop those qualities in their existing workforce. While previous research has focused on the qualities of strong leader/managers primarily in senior or first-line management positions, this book examines how successful senior, middle and first-line managers use management systems to achieve high productivity and innovation in their areas of responsibility. A qualitative research method was followed to understand how successful senior, middle and first-line managers utilize management systems to achieve their business strategy. Data were collected from historical organizational records, performance appraisals and structured, open-ended interviews

The findings suggest that managers at any level who demonstrate the ability to conceptualize, apply, and align management systems and business strategy are more likely to be considered 'successful' both in terms of performance appraisal and focal rankings. Findings also suggest the higher in one is in an organization, the greater the likelihood that one has a formal business strategy and that one or more of four management control systems are in place. Finally, this research suggests that what upper management says it desires from managers at the first-line level is not always obtained. The findings also indicate that first-line and middle managers can learn to employ effective management systems. The book concludes by suggesting a number of practical approaches learning professionals, organization development professionals and management might take to enhance the development of managers.

Managing the Business

CHAPTER 1

Introduction

The 1990s have been labeled the decade of the "learning organization" (Senge & Fulmer, 1993). Peter Senge, author of *The Fifth Discipline,* defines a learning organization as one which continually expands its capacity to create its future (1990, p. 14). The ability of an organization to learn and share what it learns quickly is viewed as a competitive advantage in a high-tech, high-change business world. Organizations recognize that managers play a critical role in an organization's ability to meet its strategic business objectives, maintain daily operations, and facilitate positive change and learning. Many researchers believe that for organizations to compete effectively they need to reexamine traditional assumptions that inform how managers learn and apply the skills and knowledge needed to excel in both tactical and strategic issues on the job (Argyris, 1993; Sayles, 1993).

STATEMENT OF THE PROBLEM

In the decade of the 1980s, American business discovered that defining the role of management as planning, organizing, controlling, coordinating and commanding was too narrow an interpretation if organizations were to compete effectively in the world market of the 1990s (Sayles, 1993). While these traditional management roles are important, additional competencies are needed in the workplace including team and leadership skills, knowledge of systems thinking, the ability to reflect critically, and the willingness to share mental models with others (Senge, 1990; Champy; 1995). Managers now have responsibility for building an environment of integrity, trust, openness and shared vision. They are expected to shift from a role in which they act as transactional managers, charged with maintaining the status quo, to transformational managers, charged with encouraging and leading dynamic change (Spreitzer & Quinn, 1996).

The inability of managers to learn and perform these new roles can be damaging to the long- and short-term efficiency, effectiveness and productivity of an organization. Clemmer (1991) observes that poor management training may lead to unsatisfactory results in areas such as providing high quality personal service, product quality, interactions with team members and employees, decision-making, and the ability to develop others. Researchers note that unsuccessful managers are often unable to assume new roles, incorporate new productive knowledge, face shortcomings, challenge mental models, share insights, accept constructive feedback, or view their work and the work of the business systemically (Deming, 1986; Schön, 1987; Senge, 1990; Clemmer, 1991; Simons, 1995). Management training that does not achieve intended results not only has negative long- and short-term effects on the organization, but is often viewed as a waste of valuable time, funding, and resources by training participants and senior management (Robinson & Robinson, 1989). Indeed, many individuals would no doubt identify with the following observation by Michael Brown,

> If, as I suggest, most of these [managerial development] programs are good, how do I not become the supermanager of my aspirations? At various times I've learned how to approach my job as a total business system, how to quantify and measure everything, how to plan strategically, how to manage change, how to manage my time, how to get results by motivating others, and umpteen other proven approaches to successful management. . . . All this leaves me confused as hell. My management instincts have been watered down. I've now been conditioned to stop in the middle of some management activity and try to remember which techniques might apply. The different management techniques seem to meld into an anti-synergistic mixture, in which the sum is less than the totality of the parts (Sandelands, 1990).

The frustration voiced by this individual at not becoming a 'supermanager' is understandable in light of the tremendous amounts of time and money spent on management and leadership development programs by organizations each year. The American Society for

Training and Development (ASTD) estimates that organizations in the United States budgeted over $59.8 billion for formal training programs in 1996 (ASTD, 1996, p. 38). Of this figure, approximately 27 percent of this budget, or $15.9 billion, was spent directly for management training (p. 46). These figures become more concrete when one considers that this equates to over 374 million hours (or almost 48 *million* man-days) in training during the calendar year (p. 54). If, as Michael Brown suggests above, much of the time spent in training is not transferring into application in the workplace, the loss in productivity on-the-job is staggering.

Some researchers stress how important the transfer of management training skills and knowledge is to the workplace. Robinson and Robinson (1989) found that managers who performed poorly after training were deficient in their ability to serve as positive role models for employees, coaches for new behaviors, reinforcers of desired behaviors on the job, and communicators of expectations regarding employee performance. In a study of 359 managers from a cross section of organizations, Robinson and Robinson reported that the major barriers to skill transfer by managers to the job included not seeing a payoff for using new skills, not having sufficient confidence to use the new skills, failing to use the skills successfully, and not seeing an immediate application for the skills (p. 117). Others found that managers who perform poorly on the job are deficient in areas such as credibility, competence, trustworthiness, and vision (Kouzes and Posner, 1993), congruence between actions and statements, micro-managers, willingness to empower, ability to measure critical business indices (Olian & Rynes, 1992), decision-making, multi-tasking (McCall & Kaplan, 1990), and leadership abilities (Bennis, 1989).

To improve manager skills and knowledge, learning professionals have generally employed traditional training and educational delivery methods for conducting management development (Marsick, 1987). These methods have consisted of providing knowledge and skill training primarily through classroom lecture, guided discussion, role-plays and media presentations of 'good' and 'bad' behavior. Management skills and knowledge are also taught in a sequence of topical subjects and skill sets that are rarely tied back to some strategic or over-arching context or model. For example, three major training vendors offer first-line management training curriculum with module topics as listed in Table 1.

Table 1: Comparison of Vendor Management Training Programs

Vendor A	Vendor B	Vendor C
• Your Role & the Basic Principles • Giving Constructive Feedback • Getting Good Information from Others • Getting Your Ideas Across • Dealing With Emotional Behavior • Recognizing Positive Results	• Perception • Organizing & Planning • Decision-making • Decisiveness • Interpersonal Relations • Leadership • Control & Follow-up • Flexibility • Oral Communications • Written Communications	• The Creative Process • Planning • Organizing • Directing • Coordinating • Delegation • Control • Decision-Making • Communication • Motivation • Inspiration

Each of these programs consists of a number of modules which offer knowledge and skills practice on specific management tasks or functions (e.g. how to make decisions, get information from others, delegate, etc.) While these approaches may be effective for teaching specific skill sets, they are not effective at helping managers understand how to apply that skill within the context of a dynamic work environment. Not surprisingly, research indicates that long-term knowledge retention and behavioral change is not always achieved using these methods (Laird, 1985). Marsick and Watkins (1990, p. 4) observe, "Employees may demonstrate that they have learned new knowledge and skills at the end of a training activity, but they find it difficult to transfer this learning to their normal work environment."

If current methods of preparing managers for their roles by focusing on teaching specific management skills are not resulting in sufficient long-term knowledge retention and behavioral change, one can surmise that a new paradigm is needed to assist managers to learn and perform on-the-job is needed. Albert Einstein observed, "The significant problems we face today cannot be solved at the same level of thinking we were at when we created them" (cited in Covey, 1989, p. 42). Accordingly, a manager should not be expected to exhibit radical changes in skill, knowledge or behavior if prompted by the same traditional training methods. Spreitzer and Quinn (1996) agree, noting that traditional approaches to management training have a limited ability to achieve behavioral change. In an extensive research effort with 3,000 Ford Motor Company managers, Spreitzer and Quinn found that an effective transformational management program would need to be designed on a new set of assumptions. Results indicated that a successful program should go beyond informing managers, to providing them with opportunities to transform themselves and their mental frame—to challenge traditional assumptions, roles, and organizational practices (Spreitzer & Quinn, 1996).

Previous Management Research

The tendency to focus on individual aspects of a manager's job by those in the training industry is reflective of traditional research approaches to studying what managers do. Several 'generations' of research have been conducted in the field of management over the past century. Some early researchers focused upon determining how to make managers more efficient by focusing on tasks or definitive work assignments (Taylor, 1911). Others focused upon describing the various 'managerial functions' that made up the totality of managerial work as they knew it (Fayol, 1930, Gulick, 1937). Later researchers worked to clarify the responsibilities inherent to the position of a managers authority (Barnard, 1938, Drucker, 1967). Still other researchers focused their attention on the experiences of individual managers, drawing from specific case studies and making generalizations associated with what successful managers do (Newcomer, 1955, Dale, 1960). More recently, scholars have explored the competencies associated with managerial success (McClelland, 1973, Klemp, 1979) while some focused on the relationship between the manager and their relationships with others (Follett, 1941; Simon, 1947). Considered as a whole, these works have attempted to develop and present the tasks, duties, functions and responsibilities of a manager. What they lack is a defining context which can assist managers to integrate the tasks, duties and responsibilities together in a rational, holistic manner that is tied to the strategic direction of the organization.

A New Context for Viewing Management

Robert Simons (1995a) offers a conceptual model (Figure 1) based on research of what excellent executive managers do. From his research on chief executives at ten Fortune 500 companies, Simons determined that excellent managers employed four systems, or 'levers of control,' to influence, align and direct the activities and attention of employees to business strategy (1995a). As Figure 1 illustrates, these four systems are (Simons, 1995b):

- Belief Systems- systems for inspiring and promoting commitment to the organization's core values.
- Boundary Systems- systems for setting limits on opportunity-seeking behavior.
- Diagnostic Control Systems- methods for monitoring goals, profitability and progress towards business targets.
- Interactive Control Systems- systems managers use to involve themselves regularly and personally in the decisions of subordinates for the purpose of stimulating organizational learning, gaining and sharing information, and focusing attention on key strategic issues.

There are several important features of this model that offer a context from which managers can apply learned management skills within a more strategic or transformational frame:

1. Each system must be aligned with and support the other systems.
2. Each system must be aligned with and support the business strategy of the organization.
3. The managerial roles, responsibilities and duties explicated by researchers can be employed within the context of the model.

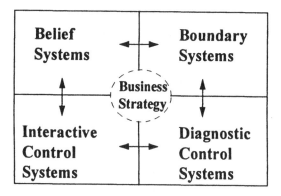

Figure 1: Model of Levers of Control

The ability to focus organizational attention on agendas linked to business strategy is the hallmark of an effective manager (Kotter, cited in Simons, 1995a). Other scholars (Bennis, 1989, McCall & Kaplan, 1990; Olian & Rynes, 1992; and Kouzes and Posner, 1993) have shown that the inability to define vision, focus employee activities and organizational resources, measure and communicate critical success factors are descriptive of poor managers. The research of Marsick (1987) and Robinson and Robinson (1989) suggests that skill and knowledge training without a context for applying the skills and knowledge is ineffective. Simons' research and subsequent model offers learning professionals and managers a context from which to apply specific and general managerial skills and knowledge in order to enhance both organizational productivity and managerial success on-the-job.

PURPOSE AND RESEARCH QUESTIONS

For organizations to enhance their effectiveness, they must continually adapt to a wide variety of unpredictable, rapid, and often erratic environmental conditions such as changes in the workforce, society, competition, technology and organizational structures. Organizations that cannot adapt to these forces will not be able to competently and effectively turn opportunities into valued services and/or products for their customers (Simons, 1995a). Managers serve a critical role as they are charged with ensuring that the organization is productive and effective (Drucker, 1986). Simon's research focusing on senior management in Fortune 500 companies, indicates that a managers' ability to balance the need for innovation and control to achieve business strategy is a crucial competency for success. His theory suggests that these senior managers achieved profitable growth by controlling the tension between creative innovation and the need for predictable goal achievement using the four 'levers,' or 'systems' of control (Simons, 1995a).

Purpose

While Simon's research indicates that excellent senior managers utilized belief, boundary, diagnostic and interactive control systems, he does not indicate the extent or amount of time these managers spent on tasks or activities related to these quadrants. Further, Simons does not indicate if or to what extent middle or first line managers utilize these systems. The purpose of the research described in this book was to explore and examine if, and to what extent successful senior, middle and first-line managers at the company used these four or similar systems of control in order to achieve high productivity and innovation in their areas of responsibility. Managers at these three levels of management in the manufacturing division of an integrated circuit manufacturer constituted the study. A stratified random sample was drawn from each of the three levels of management

Research Questions

In order to achieve the purpose of this research, the following questions were formulated in order to determine if and how successful senior, middle and first line managers in a specific integrated circuit manufacturing division apply belief, boundary, diagnostic, and interactive communication systems.

1. What belief systems undergird senior, middle and first line managers' strategy in achieving their organizational goals?
2. What boundary systems do senior, middle, and first-line managers invoke through their management strategy in order to remain focused on organizational goals?
3. What interactive control systems do senior, middle, and first-line managers employ to ensure predictable goal achievement?

4. What diagnostic control systems do senior, middle, and first-line managers use to monitor and predict quality and productivity?
5. How do senior, middle, and first-line managers use belief systems, boundary systems, interactive control systems, and diagnostic control systems to link to the business strategy of the company?

LIMITATIONS OF THE RESEARCH

A qualitative research method was determined to be the most appropriate design for obtaining an in-depth understanding of the way senior, middle and first-line managers utilized management control systems. Several factors related to sample selection and data analysis constrain this research.

The first limitation involved the use of a focused, purposeful sample selected in order to study the way senior, middle and first-line managers utilize management control systems. This sample was drawn from the manufacturing division within the company, and therefore, the descriptive data is limited in generalizability to other situations.

The second limitation of the research was the possible subjectivity and/or personal bias of the author on two levels. First, the author worked at the company, and may have induced some bias or subjectivity purely because of personal knowledge of the organization, employees and history. Efforts were made to compare and corroborate findings and observations to the raw data, findings and observations with participants, and to triangulate data with documents and observations to ensure objectivity.

A third limitation concerned the demographics of the participants. Participants in this research were drawn from an existing workforce and identified by how well they matched the criteria of 'successful manager.' The sample of participants did not reflect the general demographic mix of the American workforce or the company.

Finally, geographical, financial and time constraints prohibited a period of prolonged engagement which was recommended for qualitative research. Interviews with participants had to be kept within the bounds of availability and workload for both the participants and author.

OVERVIEW OF THE STUDY

As previously stated, the purpose of this research was to explore and examine if and to what extent successful senior, middle and first-line managers used these four or similar systems of control in order to achieve high productivity and innovation in their areas of responsibility. A review and analysis of the supporting literature relevant to this topic are presented in Chapter 2. The methods and procedures of the study are reported in Chapter 3, while the results of the research are detailed in Chapter 4. The final chapter of the study presents the summary of findings, discussion, implications and suggestions for further research.

Review of the Literature

As stated in Chapter 1, the purpose of this research is to explore and examine if and to what extent successful senior, middle and first-line managers in an organization used the four systems of control identified by Simons to achieve high productivity and innovation in their areas of responsibility. A review and analysis of the supporting literature relevant to this topic is presented in this chapter.

In this chapter, a representative sample of the primary contributors to the major models of management will be reviewed. These models include the Rational Goal Model, Internal Process Model, Human Relations Model, Behavioral Model, and Open Systems Model (Quinn, et.,al, 1996). These major contributors are described by management approach in Table 2. Particular attention will be paid to two areas. First, this chapter will focus on what these contributors say managers do in order to accomplish their job successfully. Second, how each 'generation' of management theory led to the next trend in management theory will be illustrated. A summary of each major area of management theory and description be illustrated. A summary of each major area of management theory and description of how the research of Robert Simon's builds upon previous management models will follow.

Table 2: Major Theorists by Management Model

Approach	Rational Goal Model	Internal Process Model	Human Relations Model	Behavioral Model	Open Systems Model
Theorist	Taylor Gilbreth Gantt	Fayol Follett Weber	Barnard Mayo	McGregor Maslow Herzberg	Katz & Kahn Evans & House

RATIONAL GOAL MODEL

With the coming of the industrial revolution in the late 1800s and early 1900s the study of how work was accomplished on the shop floor began with a high degree of intensity. The first major attempt to study the work environment was rational goal management which focused on how to maximize organizational productivity by improving the employee-work tool (or equipment) relationship (George, 1972). Management's role as planners and monitors of work, and the employee's role as the 'doers' of work in large factories were separated.

It was during this period that the first attempts to develop standards of production and efficient technique were attempted. These studies included looking at the effect of periodic breaks to reduce fatigue, plant layout, interactions with equipment, unnecessary motions and other factors. Stop watches and cameras were used by scientific investigators in their search for methods of maximizing efficiency.

The ultimate goal of the rational goal model was to achieve organizational effectiveness as measured by productivity and profit. These 'bottom line' ends were to be achieved by clear direction, goal clarification, rational analysis, and action taking (Quinn, et. al, 1996). In the rational goal model, management's job was seen as maximizing profit in a role of task-oriented director. Four theorists stand out as examples of the rational goal model- Frederick Taylor, Frank and Lillian Gilbreth, and Henry L. Gantt.

Frederick W. Taylor

Frederick Winslow Taylor was almost exclusively concerned with achieving efficiency through the use of time-and-motion studies, which have been referred to as "the cornerstone of scientific management" by Koontz and O'Donnell (1968, p. 20). Taylor believed that "the objective of good management was to pay high wages and have low unit production costs," and that management should remove from the shoulders of labor all "planning, organizing, controlling, determining methods, and the like..." (George, 1972, p. 92–93). Taylor maintained that inefficiency was the primary problem facing factories, and that these inefficiencies could be resolved by the application of scientific principles, thereby making management a true science (Koontz & O'Donnell, 1968). Taylor, along with many of his contemporaries, felt that 'soldiering,' or the systematic restriction of productive effort by the working class was a major cause of organizational inefficiency. "The natural laziness of men is serious," Taylor wrote, "but by far the greatest evil from which both workmen and employers are suffering is the systematic soldiering which is almost universal" (Taylor, 1911, p. 13). Drawing from his experience as the foreman for the Midvale Steel company in Philadelphia, Taylor believed that the basis of soldiering was the job control exercised by skilled workers through their expertise in the production process. Further, he felt these individuals maintained control by monopolizing skills, thereby blocking free-market forces both upon the scale of wages and employment (Green, 1983). In response, the principles embodied in scientific management broke these craft skills down into simpler, individual activities so that the skills could be learned by others.

Taylor's work led to such high perceived efficiencies that public concerns were raised that large numbers of individuals would be laid off from work. He was called before a congressional committee and testified that he believed managers should perform the following basic functions: (1) using scientific determination of the elements within a job, (2) selecting, educating and training workers scientifically, (3) cooperating with workers to implement scientific methods, and (4) dividing the responsibility for work more equitably between management and workers (Koontz & O'Donnell, 1968, p. 21). It is important to recognize that Taylor interpreted these four functions differently than we do today. Using a scientific approach to identify job elements was a means of breaking down craft skills into tasks that could be taught to anyone. Selecting, educating and training workers was a means for ensuring that unionism was avoided (Green, 1983). Cooperating meant asking workers to "do what they are told to do promptly and without asking questions or making any suggestions" (Taylor, cited in Green, 1983, p. 85). Dividing work equitably between management and workers meant vigilant supervision by management to ensure high productivity was achieved. Management, through detailed task instructions prepared each day, would be the guiding force of the organization.

Clearly, scientific management was a success as these principles offered a context to managers searching for methods to deal with labor relations at a time when higher productivity was needed. Taylor proved that the work place could be studied profitably and that standards and pay practices were important. He is also credited with developing the first systematic approach to management. Management, he believed, had its own tasks and responsibility, but could successfully cooperate with labor.

Frank & Lillian Gilbreth

Frank and Lillian Gilbreth were contemporaries of Taylor. The Gilbreths are generally acknowledged as having innovated the use of motion studies to improve worker efficiency (Montana & Charnov, 1993). Frank Gilbreth developed a classification scheme of seventeen motions used in jobs and then used this classification to analyze worker actions. He would observe and film a worker performing a task and then analyze the motions involved. When he understood all of the actions and the time it took to accomplish each action, Gilbreth would attempt to improve the efficiency of each action, thereby reducing the number of actions required to accomplish the job. The result he called job simplification. The Gilbreths were also instrumental in providing the foundation for development of meaningful work standards and incentive wage plans.

George (1972) notes that the Gilbreths work added much to the improvement of work methods, training, work environments and tools. Through the practical application of science to management, the Gilbreths were able to enhance the productivity of companies and provide a better environment for workers. George goes on to observe,

"...the Gilbreths' legacy to the development of management thought is the inculcation in the minds of managers that any and everything should be questioned as to its feasibility and applicability, and that even the new should be discarded if an improvement is in the offing" (p. 101).

Henry L. Gantt

Henry L. Gantt was an associate of Taylor at the Midvale and Bethlehem Steel Companies. Gantt made contributions in the areas of scheduling and controlling work and rewarding workers. Gantt believed that inefficiency in production was largely due to the result of management's inability to formulate realistic standards. As a result of management setting production standards too high or too low, workers were perceived as being the cause of the inefficiency.

Gantt is also credited with developing a task-and-bonus wage system. This system was based on Taylor's piece-rate system in which a worker was not guaranteed wages for substandard performance. In Gantt's task-and-wage system, if a worker completed a task for the day, the worker received a bonus in addition to their regular pay for the day. If the worker did not complete the task, they would only receive their regular pay for the day without any penalty (George, 1972).

As with Taylor and the Gilbreths, Gantt believed that management should use scientific data to improve efficiency. Further, he felt that realistic work standards should be determined by observation and measurement. Montana and Charnov (1993) note that Gantt believed that work could be scheduled only when the nature of the work and the amount of work to be done had be clearly identified. Gantt is also acknowledged for his emphasis on management's responsibility to train and equip workers appropriately, to form better work habits, and be more productive.

Rational Goal Model Summary

The intent of rational goal management was to maximize productivity by improving the employee-work tool relationship. Taylor, the Gilbreths, and Gantt provided the foundations for using scientific methods for determining how to improve worker productivity. Some primary roles and practices of managers using the principles of scientific management are described in Table 3.

While advocates of the rational goal model sought to achieve organizational effectiveness as measured by productivity and profit, and viewed management's job serving in the role of task-oriented director, others began to feel that this single-minded focus on improving productivity was not sufficient. As a result, a second model of management began to form based on the idea that management should also be responsible for developing stable routines and procedures through planning and control (Natemeyer, 1978). This model became known as the internal process model.

Table 3: Rational Goal Roles & Practices

Management's Role	• Use scientific methods to determine elements within a job • Select, educate and train workers scientifically • Cooperate with workers to implement scientific methods • Divide the responsibility for work equitably between management and workers
Examples of What Managers Do	• Time & motion studies • Planning • Establish detailed task instructions • Monitor work • Worker selection • Job determination • Standardization of tools & implements of work

INTERNAL PROCESS MODEL

Like the Rational Goal Model, the Internal Process Model was also a means-ends management model. A major difference was that this model is based on the belief that routinization leads to stability. Theorists that typify the internal process model include Henri Fayol, Mary Parker Follett, and Max Weber. These theorists emphasized process such as the definition of responsibilities, measurement, documentation and record keeping. Control over employee production and efficiency was achieved by the application of policies and procedures. Managers played a role of serving as technical expert, work-flow monitor, and work coordinator.

Henri Fayol

Henri Fayol published the earliest comprehensive general theory of management (George, 1972). Fayol's early work was enthusiastically utilized in Europe, but was not widely accepted in the United States until the publication of *General and Industrial Management* in 1949.

Fayol and Taylor differed in the perspective from which they viewed the problem of improving efficiency in the work place. Taylor's approach was to address the problem from a technical point of view beginning at the shop floor, and working his way up. Fayol's approach was to address the problem from a broader perspective beginning at the company board-of-director's, and work his way down. George notes that "Taylor's approach to management dealt with specifics of job analysis, employee's motions, and time standards; while Fayol viewed management as a teachable theory dealing with planning, organizing, commanding, coordinating and controlling" (p. 111).

Fayol felt that management was an activity that all humans undertook regardless of the setting. Given this perspective, Fayol believed that everyone could benefit from learning a general knowledge of management. The six functions of management identified by Fayol (George, 1968, p. 112–113) included:

- Planning- examining the future and drawing up a plan of action.
- Organizing- building up a dual structure (human and material) to achieve the undertaking.
- Commanding- maintaining activity among the personnel of the organization.
- Coordinating- establishing a formal structure of authority through which work is arranged, defined and coordinated.
- Controlling- seeing that everything is accomplished in conformity with the established plan and command.
- Staffing- bringing in and training work place employees and maintaining favorable conditions for work.

In addition to these six functions of management, Fayol developed fourteen principles which he felt could guide managers in resolving work-related problems. The fourteen principles listed below, in Fayol's mind, would provide managers with the skills and abilities they needed to perform their role. Fayol's fourteen management principles were (Montana & Charnov, 1993):

1. Division of labor- Work is separated into its basic tasks and divided between individual workers or work groups that can specialize in the specific task, leading to work specialization.
2. Authority- The legitimate right to exercise power within the organization to obtain worker obedience.
3. Discipline- The application of punishment for failure to act in accord with the desires of those who possess legitimate authority in the organization.
4. Unity of command- A worker should receive orders only from one manager in order to minimize conflict and promote clear communication.
5. Unity of direction- The whole organization should have one common goal and seek to accomplish that goal in all its activities.
6. Subordination of the individual- The goals of the organization are more important than the personal goals of the individual worker.
7. Remuneration- Each employee should receive compensation based on a formula that is applied to all employees.
8. Centralization- Subordinates should be delegated just enough responsibility and authority to establish the assigned task.
9. Scalar chain- Managers and employees in an organization should exist in a chain of command that is hierarchical.
10. Order- The resources of the organization must be in the right place at the right time.
11. Equity- Employees should be treated equally and fairly.
12. Stability of personnel- Skilled, successful employees are a valuable resource to an organization, and retention of these individuals should be a priority.
13. Initiative- Management should encourage employees to seek greater self-motivated work undertaken for the good of the company.
14. Esprit de corps- Management should try to encourage harmony and good relations among employees.

It is important to note that Fayol believed that the functions and principles of management could be learned, and lobbied to have them included in curricula of business schools. Fayol's contribution to the field is important in that he presented the first concept of management as a separate form of knowledge applicable to all human activity, the first comprehensive theory of management, and the concept of teaching and developing a curricula for managers.

Mary Parker Follett

Mary Parker Follett believed that work should be a partnership between management and workers and that management should derive its power from superior knowledge and expertise, not solely from authority (Stoner & Wankel, 1986). She looked at both the social and group aspects of working noting that managers had to deal with the motivations and desires of both the individual and group.

Follett observed that the motivations of an individual on the job are the same as those that motivate them at home. As a result, she suggested that organizations needed to coordinate group effort to achieve the most efficient effort towards task completion. She also viewed power, leadership and authority as dynamic concepts for improving cooperation and productivity, and believed that leaders were not born, but could be developed through proper education in group dynamics and human behavior (George, 1972). Follett perceived coordination as the primary function of management and identified four of its elements: (1) coordination by direct contact with people concerned, (2) coordination that is a continuous process, (3) coordination found in the initial stages of an endeavor, and (4) coordination as a reciprocal relation of all aspects of a situation (Follett, 1941). Mary Parker Follett played a crucial role in bridging the gap between Taylor's scientific management focus on the individual and an approach focusing on human behavior.

Max Weber

Max Weber was a German sociologist-philosopher who had an interest in the process of social change and the effect of rationality on religious thought and capitalism (Huczynski, 1996). Weber was intrigued with the idea of determining a mode of organization in which goals were clearly determined and in which all conduct that was extemporaneous to the goal was eliminated.

Weber identified five elements which, if implemented within an organization, would serve as a blueprint for rationally designed organizations in which rational individuals carried out their work. These elements were division of labor and specialization, impersonal orientation, hierarchy of authority, rules and regulations, and career orientation (Hoy & Miskel, 1991).

Weber defined division of labor and specialization as the method by which various work tasks and activities were divided up within the organization. Weber recognized that the tasks that needed to be accomplished in most organizations were too complex for one individual. He felt that division of labor among other individuals and units improved efficiency. Division of labor led to increased specialization because efficiency would improve, leading to employees who became more expert in their work.

Weber also felt that in the ideal organization, employees would make decisions and take actions based on facts, not emotions. He reasoned that the working environment of a bureaucratic organization should provide an impersonality based "without hatred or passion, and hence without affection or enthusiasm (Weber, 1947, p. 331). The intent of the impersonal orientation of organizations was to ensure equality of treatment and to facilitate rational behavior.

Weber also advocated for a system of rules which would cover the rights and duties of each employee (Weber, 1947). By developing a system of policies, procedures, and job descriptions, management could ensure continuity of operations, and uniformity in the application of discipline, hiring, promotion and termination of employees.

Bureaucratic organizations, according to Weber, would be arranged hierarchically with a rigid system of control and supervision of one office by another. This feature can be easily seen in most organizational charts, in which their is a clear line of authority which runs from the top of the pyramid down to the lowest level. The intent of a clear hierarchy of authority is to guarantee compliance to orders from senior staff down to lower level employees.

To encourage loyalty within an organization, Weber maintained that employees be of encourage them to remain with the organization by providing systems or tenure and long term service agreements.

These systems would also be helpful in promoting individuals by means of seniority and achievement.

While many of Weber's views are close to those of scientific management, his work on authority and bureaucracy provided human relations and behavioral model theorists with the starting point in their beliefs regarding organizations as social systems that interact with and are dependent on their surrounding environment.

Internal Process Model Summary

Theorists reflective of the internal process model emphasized the definition of responsibilities, measurement, documentation, and record keeping as major management responsibilities. Some of the major roles and practices of managers within this framework are described in Table 4. Proponents of the internal process model believed that control over employee production and efficiency could be achieved by the application of policies and procedures.

Table 4: Internal Process Roles & Practices

Management's Role	• Planning • Organizing • Commanding • Coordinating • Controlling
Examples of What Managers Do	• Developing plans of action • Ensuring plans of action are carried out • Selection of personnel • Fair compensation for work • Eliminating the incompetent • Be a good model for employees • Coordinate activity and resources

Managers within this paradigm would play the role of serving as a technical expert, work-flow monitor, and work-flow coordinator. Towards the middle of the century, a third model of management began to develop. Adherents of this model believed that management was more than reaching higher productivity through scientific methods or routines. Rather, these theorists viewed management as a process of getting things done through and with people operating in organized groups (Koontz, 1961). This model became known as the Human Relations Model.

HUMAN RELATIONS MODEL

The human relations movement is also known as the organic or humanistic approach (Griffin, 1987). Chester Barnard and Elton Mayo are two individuals who are representative of this movement. The human relations approach was concerned with how managers and workers related. Adherents of this model suggested that human relations can be characterized as good or bad depending on the quality of that relationship.

In popular management mythology, human relations comes down to 'being nice to workers.' Reduced to its essentials, the human relations message is characterized by six propositions:

1. A focus on people, rather than upon mechanics or economics.
2. People exist in an organizational environment rather than an unorganized social context.
3. A key activity in human relations is motivating people.
4. Motivation should be directed towards teamwork requiring the coordination and the cooperation of the individuals involved.
5. Human relations, through teamwork, seeks to fulfill both individual and organizational objectives simultaneously.
6. Both individuals and organizations share a desire for efficiency, and try to achieve maximum results with minimum inputs.

The underlying assumption of the human relations movement then, was that good human relations will lead to higher productivity, lower absenteeism, etc.

Chester Barnard

Chester I. Barnard was President of the New Jersey Bell Telephone company. In his 1938 book *The Functions of the Executive*, Barnard brought what could be termed a pragmatic approach to management that reflected his experience as a practicing manager attempting to improve organizational effectiveness. He defined effectiveness as the degree of accomplishment of recognized objectives through cooperative action (1938, p. 55). Barnard's work also pointed to the significance of the informal organization and the fact that informal relationships, if managed properly, could be powerful tools for the manager. In Barnard's view, an organization was responsible for blending the needs of the worker with the goals of the organization. He recognized that organizations also had groups of workers that acted as informal organizations themselves and could be used to reach the organization's formal goals.

Barnard defined the essential functions of a manager as: (1) providing a system of communication; (2) promoting the securing of essential efforts; (3) formulating and defining organizational purpose (1938, p. 217). Barnard also felt that managerial work was extremely complex, and that simply viewing management's job as "to manage a group of persons," as too narrow a definition (p. 216). He stressed that managers should induce workers to cooperate and while this inducement could take the form of an order, that a cooperative and productive relationship could best be obtained if the manager ensured the worker (1) understood the reason for the order, (2) believed it to be consistent with the purposes of the organization, (3) believed it to be consistent with their own personal interests, and (4) were able to comply with the order (George, p. 141).

Barnard differed from Taylor and Fayol in a number of areas. Where Taylor concentrated on improving the task efficiency of the individual, Fayol focused on the principles of management, managerial functions, and responsibilities. Barnard, on the other hand, focused on analyzing "the kinds and qualities of forces at work and the manner of their interactions" (p. 141). In other words, Barnard began with the individual worker, transitioned to the need for a cooperative organized approach, and ended with the need for well understood managerial functions.

Elton Mayo

The human relations movement drew heavily for its academic basis on a series of famous experiments known as the Hawthorn studies. The Hawthorn studies refer to a series of research projects which began in 1924 at the Hawthorn plant of the Western Electric company located outside of Chicago. The aim of the research effort was to examine the relationship between working conditions and output.

At the beginning of the Hawthorn studies, the investigators adopted a physiological approach which involved manipulating the lighting in the work area. Early results, however, suggested that variables such as lighting could not be treated independently of the meanings that workers gave to those variables. The researchers concluded that economic motives were relatively unimportant in motivating workers and in raising productivity. Rather, they argued, solidarity and affiliation was the key.

The growth of human relations was fostered by the problem of motivating or persuading employees to share the goals of the organization. When Mayo addressed the problem of workers not behaving in the way management would prefer, he concluded the way to deal with this difficulty was to retain both hierarchy and specialization while forming the equivalent of the 'family' in the workplace. Authoritarianism would remain but would take the guise of a paternalistic interest in the worker who, in turn, would respond in a respectful manner. Viewing the organization as a family gave justification to treating competition between departments or divisions as something to be avoided.

Human Relations Model Summary

The human relations model appealed to managers as it offered a framework of scientific evidence in support of the most satisfactory (managerial) conclusion that "the requisite skills could release the enthusiasm for cooperation with management which work groups possessed as the result of their deep-felt need for belonging" (Child 1969). Some major roles and practices of managers reflective of this model are described in Table 5.

Human relations theorists viewed management as a process of getting things done through others operating in organized groups. This view provided the framework for the behavioral model of management. Proponents of this view put forth the argument that since managing involves "getting things done with and through people, the study of management must be centered on interpersonal relations (Koontz, cited in Natemeyer, 1978, p. 22).

Table 5: Human Relations Roles & Practices

Management's Role	• Blend worker needs with the needs of the organization. • Build good relationships with workers in order to improve productivity, morale, etc. • Improve the workplace environment
Examples of What Managers Do	• Communicate organization goals to workers • Ensure workers understand the reasons for their work • Reward workers for achieving goals • Work to enhance work-group interaction • Decision-making

BEHAVIORAL MODEL

The next management model stressed that for managers to get work accomplished through people, the study of management must be centered around the workers, their interpersonal relations, worker motivation, group dynamics, individual drives, and group relations (George, 1972). Key contributors to this school of thought included Douglas McGregor, Abraham Maslow and Frederick Herzberg.

Douglas McGregor

Douglas McGregor is known for his theory X and theory Y models which provide a framework for understanding a managers mind-set (McGregor, 1960). McGregor reasoned that workers had spent decades adapting to the scientific management approach exemplified by external control over their work methods, tools, output and pace (Weisbord, 1989). He further believed that workers would prefer a different relationship with management. From these beliefs came McGregor's Theory X and Theory Y management models.

McGregor suggested that a manager with a mind-set of Theory X assumed that workers were not very bright, lazy, slothful, gullible, needed direction, and disliked responsibility. McGregor suggested that managers, through the organizational structure, policies, and procedures, reinforce this view. Theory Y managers, on the other hand, viewed workers as motivated to work, willing to take responsibility, and not gullible or unintelligent. Theory Y managers assumed that given a chance, workers were capable and even interested in furthering the organization's goals.

Contrary to the conclusions of some other management theorists, McGregor did not feel that there was any best way or style to manage. Rather, that successful managers were those who had a clear sense of direction and flexible repertoire of behaviors from which to draw upon. Effective managers, according to McGregor, were able to listen, delegate and involve others, *and* decide and direct (Weisbord, 1989). McGregor said, "The essential task of management is to arrange the organizational conditions and methods of operation so that people can achieve their own goals best by directing their own efforts towards organizational objectives" (McGregor, 1957, p. 26). Theory Y, he argued, implied a system of management, and that no single technique could ever embody a managers mental map of reality.

Abraham Maslow

Maslow (1943) presented his theory of human motivation based on a hierarchy of five sets of needs. These needs were arranged in a hierarchy ranging from physiological to safety, social, ego and self-actualization needs. It is interesting to note that the theory itself was never conceived with management or organizations in mind. In his original writings, Maslow addressed social issues in terms of the effect of societal factors upon the mental health of individuals. He wrote that his book expounding his ideas was in the realm of science or pre-science, rather than a personal or management philosophy (Huczynski, 1996).

At the first level in his hierarchy, Maslow identified physiological needs, which consisted of the basic biological functions of human beings such as hunger, thirst, sleep and sex. The second level consisted of safety and security needs, or the need for a safe, secure environment. Love and social needs comprised the third level, or the need for belonging and connection to others. At the fourth level were esteem needs, or the need to be regarded well in terms or achievement accomplishment and recognition. The final level, self-actualization, was a result of the discontent people felt if they were not doing what they were best suited for, fulfilling life goals and to realizing their potential (Campbell & Pritchard, 1976).

Maslow hypothesized that, on average, the physiological needs of human beings were generally 85 per cent satisfied, the safety needs 70 per cent satisfied, the social needs 50 per cent satisfied, ego needs 40 per cent satisfied, and the self-actualization needs 10 per cent satisfied (Huczynski, 1996). Maslow also noted that only unsatisfied needs in the individual acted as motivators. He proposed that while the needs could be considered in a loose, step-wise progression, it was possible for higher level needs to emerge at some point prior to the total satisfaction of the lower level needs.

Maslow's needs hierarchy theory has been widely taught to managers, and has been used to guide decisions about employees (Matheson, 1974) and about how organizations should be managed (Clark, 1960). Except for the case of the need for self-actualization, many managers misunderstand that Maslow's theory does not stress individual differences, and does not require the measurement of individual motivational patterns before action is taken. Huczynski notes that one of the reasons Maslow's theory appeals to managers is the "if-then" propositions:

> The theory implies that, to the extent that management could control conditions in the workgroup's environment, it could induce certain motivational patterns and obtain the benefits of increased production output and reduced turnover and absenteeism. The theory also includes 'when-then' propositions. For example, *when* job conditions are poor in terms of pay and security, *then* employees will focus attention on the work itself, *so then, if* management wishes to obtain significant motivational consequences, it has to change these work conditions. Similarly *when job* conditions improve, *then* the behavior of the supervisors become important, so *then* management needs to train them. *When* the Job conditions improve still further, *then* the role of the supervisor becomes less important and the work itself re-establishes its importance as a motivator. Finally, *when* people move up the needs hierarchy, *then* they will become motivated only by the higher level needs (1996, p. 24).

Because it has often been presented as a formula for 'good' management practice (i.e. design your organization and managerial strategies to encourage self-actualization and the people will voluntarily integrate their own goals with those of the organization), Maslow's hierarchy of needs continues to permeate much of the training offered to managers and others concerning motivation at work.

Frederick Herzberg

Frederick Herzberg is known for the Motivation-Hygiene theory- also called the two-factor or dual-factor theory (Herzberg, 1959). In developing his theory, Herzberg used a critical incident methodology to study accountants and engineers to determine what events they experienced at work that resulted in a significant improvement or reduction in their job satisfaction. As a result of this research, Herzberg identified two sets of variables or factors he believed accounted for most worker motivation. Variables which acted to enhance motivation included achievement, recognition, the work itself, responsibility and advancement. Herzberg noted that when the motivators were not fulfilled, only minimal dissatisfaction occurred. Hygiene factors were those which created dissatisfaction on the job if not fulfilled. These factors included salary, the chance for personal growth, relationships with subordinates, peers and superiors, status, level of supervision, the organization's policies and procedures, working conditions, personal life and level of job security (p. 72).

Herzberg's contribution to management thinking derives in part from his theory that two sets of variables, hygiene factors and motivators, together influenced worker motivation, and partly from his concept of job enrichment (Brown, 1980). While Herzberg did not say that hygiene factors were less important than motivators, as with Maslow's theory, many managers misinterpreted the theory to say that investments in salary, fringe benefits and working conditions could yield only limited results (Huczynski, 1996).

The job enrichment approach, which was initially developed from Herzberg's work, maintained that workers could be motivated by positive job-related experiences and by providing employees with more control over their job tasks. Lupton described Herzberg's ideas in the following way:

> If you wish (as employer or manager) to have an efficient organization, you must set to work to improve the performance of the individuals who presently work for it. It does not matter who the individuals are, what they can do, what they are doing, what the organization does, how it does it, or what it is, there will always be scope for re-dividing and re-designing its tasks so as to enrich them, and for so arranging the context of administrative procedure,

> supervision and interpersonal relationships, that they will not inhibit
> motivation and satisfaction.
>
> (Lupton 1976: 123)

The Lupton quotation clearly signals the universality and the appeal to managers of the idea of applying Herzberg's theory and the concept of job enrichment on-the-job. Herzberg's theory stressed only two types of motivation variables and thus was easy to communicate to managers. In addition, his theory prescribed a set of simple steps through which the technique of job enrichment could be applied. Blackler and Shimmin (1984) observed that the fascination which the theory possessed for many managers was that it provided basic, easy-to-follow, guiding principles for action.

It may be that the popularity of the motivation-hygiene theory, and particularly the idea-technique of job enrichment, stemmed from the fact that it provided managers with the results they wanted. However, the results may not have been in the area of increased productivity and product quality. Empirical research studies showed two things. First, that a great deal more was written and talked about job enrichment than was actually put into practice. Fincham and Rhodes (1988) reported that there was widespread acceptance of work humanization at the level of public policy. However, the true impact on the shop floor was far less significant (Wall, 1982). Fincham and Rhodes (1988) also reported that a number of experiments which claimed far-reaching job enrichment results involved only cosmetic changes, and that only half of the workers interviewed were aware that any change had taken place, and only a small proportion of these identified the changes as either positive or significant.

Behavioral Model Summary

The behavioral management model stressed that for managers to get work accomplished through people, the study of management must be centered around the workers and their interpersonal relations including worker motivation, group dynamics, individual drives, and group relations. Some of the management roles and practices which are reflective of this view are described in Table 6. Where the behavioral model focused on interpersonal relationships, the next model grew out of the recognition that organizations and employees did not operate in closed systems. In the open systems model the organization is faced with a need to compete in an ambiguous as well as competitive environment in which key criteria for organizational effectiveness were adaptability and external support.

Table 6: Behavioral Roles & Practices

Management's Role	• Capitalize on workers innate interest and willingness to further company goals • Modify organizational structure, policies and procedures to support employee initiative • Consider employee needs • Enrich jobs as needed
Examples of What Managers Do	• Determine what motivates employees • Provide opportunities for personal growth • Provide direction • Adapt leadership & management style to the situation • Listen • Delegate effectively • Involve workers in decision-making

OPEN SYSTEMS MODEL

In the mid-sixties, the ever-increasing rate of change and the need to understand how to manage in a fast-changing, knowledge-intensive world led to the development of the open systems model of organization. These theorists included Katz and Kahn at the University of Michigan and House and Evans at Southern Illinois University. The open systems model was more dynamic than previous models in that the manager was no longer seen as a rational decision maker controlling a machinelike organization. Open systems theory suggested that in contrast to the highly systematic principles proposed previous models, managers live in highly unpredictable environments and have little time to organize and plan. They are, instead, bombarded by constant stimuli and forced to make rapid decisions. Such observations were consistent with the movement to develop contingency theories which also recognized the simplicity of earlier approaches (Morgan, 1986).

In the open systems model the organization is faced with a need to compete in an ambiguous as well as competitive environment in which the key criteria for organizational effectiveness were adaptability and external support. The assumption underlying the open systems model is that continual adaptation and innovation lead to the acquisition and maintenance of external resources. The organization was perceived to need more of an innovative climate or "adhocracy" than a bureaucracy. In an open systems organization, common vision and shared values are very important. Here, if an employee's efficiency declines, it may be seen as a result of long periods of intense work, an overload of stress, and perhaps a case of burnout. The manager is expected to be a creative innovator and a someone who is able to use power and influence in the organization effectively within the organization.

Daniel Katz & Robert Kahn

Daniel Katz and Robert Kahn were two of the early writers on the subject of open systems. Katz and Kahn noted that social organizations are open systems made up of the patterned activities of the organization's members (1966). Organizations, they defined as "energetic input-output systems in which the energetic return from the output reactivates the system" (p. 16). They also observed that the two fundamental criteria for identifying their functions were:

- tracing the pattern of energy exchange or activity of people as it results in some output and,
- ascertaining how the output is translated into energy which reactivates the pattern (p. 18).

Katz and Kahn's contribution to management stems from their admonition to managers that the organization cannot be understood apart from its environment. They stated that traditional closed models of management tended to view the organization and its activities as separate and independent from the external environment. Open systems, on the other hand, cannot be understood without also understanding all internal and external environmental forces acting upon it. Katz and Kahn note that managers who persist in viewing organizations as closed systems fail to develop adequate feedback systems for accounting for all of the forces and dynamics which act upon and influence the activities and processes of the organization.

Katz and Kahn identified nine characteristics which they believed defined open systems. These were importation of energy, through-put, output, systems as cycles of events, negative entropy, information input-negative feedback, the steady state and dynamic homeostasis, differentiation, and equifinality (1966). Katz and Kahn also observed that managers that do not consider these characteristics frequently attempt to enact organizational change efforts by focusing too specifically, such as when they try to change individuals without considering the systems in which the individuals operate. They noted, "attempts to change organizations by changing individuals have a long history of theoretical inadequacy and practical failure" (1978, p. 658). Simplified approaches to change management without full consideration of the employees, organizational characteristics and external environment, they assert, is not sufficient. Scott (1981)also agreed noting that the open systems model stresses the reciprocal ties that bind and interrelate the organization with those elements that surround and penetrate it. The environment is perceived to be the ultimate source of materials, energy, and information" (p. 119–120).

Even if managers considered the external environment, organizational sources of resistance to change might occur. For example, Katz and Kahn observed that the purposes and goals of the organization may not reflect the purposes and goals of the individual members. As a result, attempts to change may be met with six major sources of resistance. First among these is over-determination, or the organization's own structure an systems providing resistance to change as they are designed to maintain stability. Second, a narrow focus of change may not account for the many interdependencies among organizational elements. Third, the employees themselves may resist change through entrenched group norms. Fourth, some may resist change because they see the change as a threat to their expertise, or fifth, to their power. Finally, any group that is currently satisfied with current resource allocations may resist change if they feel that allocation may be diminished.

Organizations and the managers within organizations, Katz and Kahn maintained, need to understand these characteristics in their planning, coordination, and activities. Failure to do so would directly affect the success of the organization since the organization is dependent on, and influenced by, the external environment.

Robert J. House & Martin G. Evans

Martin G. Evans (1970) and Robert J. House (1971) are credited with development of another systems approach to management and leadership effectiveness. The path-goal theory of leadership explains how leaders or managers influence worker perceptions of work goals, personal goals, and the path taken to achieve those goals (House, 1971). The theory maintains that workers will be motivated to perform a job if (Montana & Charnov, 1996, p. 229):

- he or she believes that the job can be accomplished (expectancy)
- the rewards offered are suitable for the task needing to be accomplished (instrumentality), and
- the rewards are meaningful to the individual (valence).

When expectancy, instrumentality and valence are high, House and Evans maintain that the motivation to accomplish the job will be high. The manager or leader is very instrumental in affecting these variables as they influence employee behavior by clarifying the behaviors (or the path) that lead to the desired results (or goals).

The path-goal theory is considered an open systems model as it considers a number of variables that influence the process. First, the leaders' behavioral approach is considered. The four basic types of leadership behavior House and Mitchell identify include a directive, achievement-oriented, supportive or participative approach (1975). The leader chooses a leadership style to match a particular situation. Types of situational factors which must be considered include personal characteristics of the subordinates and environmental factors. Personal characteristics include personal needs, locus of control, and perceived ability. Environmental factors include task structure, degree of formalization, and the norms of the primary work group. Together, the leader behavior and situational factors combine to influence the effectiveness of the work group as defined by the level of employee job satisfaction and motivation. Effective managers then, are able to lead their employees when the manager's behavior provides the employees with the direction and rewards necessary to ensure job satisfaction and high performance (Hoy and Miskel, 1993).

The main contribution of the Path-Goal Theory is to point to the need for managers to understand or diagnose their work situation more effectively before taking action. This model suggests that managers should consider their own personal behavior, the internal and external environment and the needs and characteristics of the employees must all be considered. How these elements interrelate and influence one another should be a major part of the conceptualization and action-planning of managers.

Open Systems Model Summary

In the open systems model the organization faces a need to compete in an ambiguous as well as competitive environment where key criteria for organizational effectiveness are adaptability and external support. Table 7 illustrates some of the roles and practices that characterize managers operating from within this model.

Table 7: Open Systems Roles & Practices

Management's Role	• Consider internal & external factors influencing the organization • Develop shared vision, values & goals • Develop work environment adaptive to change • Develop internal & external feedback mechanisms
Examples of What Managers Do	• Obtain employee participation in the development of vision, values & goals • Encourage creativity & initiative • Help define work boundaries • Communicate internal & external factors influencing organization • Build cross-functional relationships • Maintain systems perspective when planning and coordinating activities

The assumption underlying the open systems model is that continual adaptation and innovation lead to the acquisition and maintenance of external resources.

ROBERT SIMONS MANAGEMENT SYSTEMS MODEL

Robert Simons (1995a) offers a conceptual model based on research into what excellent executive managers do to achieve their business strategy. From his research on chief executives at ten Fortune 500 companies, Simons determined that each employed four systems which served as a context for influencing, aligning and directing the activities and attention of employees to achieve business strategy (1995a).

Simons defines management control systems as "the formalized procedures and systems that use information to maintain or alter patterns in organizational activity" (1990, p. 128) These controls may include planning, budgeting, environmental scanning, competitor analysis, performance reporting and evaluation, resource allocation, and employee recognition systems. He notes that the power these systems bring to senior management stems from the ability to assist these individuals in four areas (1995b). First, managers do not have the time or capacity to process all of the information available to them. Without the proper amount of organizational attention, new and innovative products and solutions cannot be developed. The four systems help the individual to ensure that organizational attention is focused on the goals with the greatest benefit to its business strategy. Second, senior managers report that they are faced with a myriad of external strategic uncertainties that may impact their business. Strategic uncertainties are defined as "the uncertainties and contingencies that could threaten or invalidate the current strategy of the business" (p. 94). While the strategic uncertainties for different businesses may vary depending on factors such as market strategy, competition, and resource availability, managers must have a system for providing information needed to ensure the organization is focusing on variables critical to its survival. Third, senior managers need to be able to communicate the values, purpose and direction of the organization. The four systems provide a framework for achieving this goal. Finally, senior managers report the need for a mechanism for monitoring how the organization is doing in the short and long term. Simons model provides the context from performance variables that are critical to the organization's success can be monitored and reported. The relationships between the systems and these four problem areas are illustrated in Figure 2. Each of the four systems will be discussed in the paragraphs that follow.

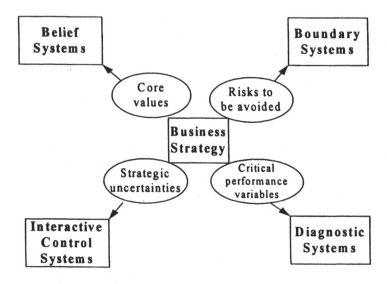

Figure 2: Systems & Business Strategy Relationship

Belief Systems

All organizations are created for a purpose. Simons notes that an organization's belief system is "the explicit set of organizational definitions that senior managers communicate formally and reinforce systematically to provide basic values, purpose and direction for the organization" (p. 34). Belief systems convey the core values of the company and those within the company (Table 8). While the systems may be created through vision or mission statements, credos or statements of purpose, it is through the application of these beliefs that they either become real, or perceived as a facade. Feldman and March have shown that belief systems must be perceived as valid and real if they are to inspire and guide the organization in the process of discovery (1981, p. 180).

Ashforth and Mael (cited in Simons, 1995b, p. 37) note that as a business grows, or the opportunity for service expands, the creation and communication of a belief systems increases in importance. They observe that managers can define and direction of organizational initiatives by (1) asserting uniqueness, (2) making it prestigious to be a member of the group, and (3) using the formal beliefs as symbols of what the organization represents. By employing these types of initiatives in the development and implementation of strong belief systems, managers can increase employee commitment, provide organizational stability, and reinforce the uniqueness of the organization in the eyes of its employees and customers (Mink, Owen & Mink, 1993; Block, 1993).

Table 8: Belief Systems

What	An explicit set of beliefs that define basic values, purpose and direction, including how value is created; level of desired performance; and human relationships
Why	To provide momentum and guidance to opportunity-seeking behavior
How	Mission statements Vision statements Credos Statements of purpose
When	When opportunities to expand dramatically occur When top management desires to change strategic direction When top managers desire to energize the workforce
Who	Senior managers personally write substantive drafts Staff groups facilitate communication, feedback and awareness

Boundary Systems

The second system identified by Simons identifies the playing field, or boundaries within which the organization's members should focus their efforts. Simons notes that individuals and organizations are opportunity-seekers; that they tend to continually search for new and better ways to overcome obstacles, improve products, processes and create value (1995b, p. 39). Boundaries, (see Table 9), define the rules and limits to opportunity-seeking behavior. In essence, these provide the mechanism for ensuring that the organization and its member do not waste their energy (consciously or unconsciously) in the pursuit of opportunities that lie outside the strategic direction or business plan. Simons observes:

> The belief systems provides organizational purpose and momentum to guide and motivate individual opportunity-seeking within

unlimited opportunity space. With the belief systems, boundary systems communicate the acceptable domain for search activity and thereby demarcate the opportunity domain as a subset of opportunity space within which organizational participants can exercise their energy. Beliefs systems and boundary systems transform unbounded opportunity space into a focused domain that organizational participants can be encouraged to exploit (p. 41).

Table 9: Boundary Systems

What	Formally stated rules, limits and proscriptions tied to defined sanctions and credible threats of punishment
Why	To allow the greatest individual creativity within defined limits or freedom
How	Codes of business conduct
	Strategic planning systems
	Asset acquisition systems
	Operational guidelines
When	Business conduct boundaries- use when reputation costs are high
	Strategic boundaries- use when excessive search and experimentation risks dissipating the resources and energy of the organization
Who	Senior managers formulate with the assistance of staff experts
	Staff groups monitor compliance

By providing the motivation and purpose to guide workers through a strong belief system, and clear boundaries through policies, procedures, codes of conduct and operational guidelines, managers have more leverage from which to delegate. Boundaries, like the rules and playing field in a football game, are stated in terms of what employees should *not* do. By specifying the limits, either at a strategic level (5–year plan) or individual level (codes of employee behavior), subordinates may use the limits of their creativity to find new ways of creating added value for the organization.

Several researchers have noted that boundaries must have credible sanctions if they are to be believed and followed (Coleman, 1990; Lorange & Morton, 1974). In dynamic and competitive environments, highly motivated and well-intended individuals may be pressured to behave in ways or take actions that the organization's belief systems and boundaries define as unacceptable. Credible, clear sanctions provide a balance against this type of activity. By the same token,

Simons also notes that if boundaries are too restrictive or oppressive, individual creativity, initiative, and motivation will be stifled (1995a, p. 54). It is a paradox that a delicate tension exists between beliefs and boundaries that provides employees the greatest amount of commitment, motivation, empowerment, and freedom to contribute to the organization (Simons, 1994).

Diagnostic Systems

The third system within Simons' model is the diagnostic system intended to allow management to monitor organizational outcomes and to correct deviations from predetermined standards of performance (1995a). The three essential characteristics of a diagnostic system that Simons identifies are (1) the ability to measure the outputs of a process, (2) the existence of predetermined standards against which actual results can be compared, and (3) the ability to correct deviations from the standard (p. 59). Examples of diagnostic systems within an organization include goals, objectives, business plans, budgets, project plans, and human resource staffing plans. As described in Table 10, diagnostic systems can be powerful tools for ensuring alignment to the organization's business strategy.

Scholars have noted the importance of measurement in ensuring that an organization's intended business strategy is being followed (Mintzberg, 1979; Merchant, 1985). By identifying critical performance variables, management can monitor and respond to information that indicates that action is warranted. Simons defines critical performance variables as those "which must be achieved or implemented successfully for the intended strategy of the business to succeed" (p. 63). He goes on to note that one way to identify critical performance variables is to imagine that the organization's strategy has failed, and ask what factors would be identified as caused for the failure.

Table 10: Diagnostic Systems

What	Feedback systems that monitor organizational outcomes and correct deviations from preset standards of performance
Why	To allow effective resource allocation
	To define goals
	To provide motivation
	To establish guidelines for evaluation & corrective action
	To free scarce management attention
How	Set standards (Goals and objectives, project monitoring systems, brand revenue systems, strategic planning systems)
	Measure outputs (Profit plans and budget forecasts)
	Link incentives to goal achievement (Sales, service, production goals)
When	Performance standards can be preset
	Outputs can be measured
	Feedback used to influence or correct deviations from desired standard
	Process or output is a critical performance variable
Who	Senior managers negotiate goals, receive and review exception reports, and follow-up on significant exceptions
	Staff groups maintain diagnostic systems, gather data, and prepare exception reports

As with belief and boundary systems, effective diagnostic systems allow the maximum amount of empowerment, motivation and autonomy to individuals in an organization. Simons observes that for diagnostic systems to be most effective, managers must invest their attention to the system in three instances. First, managers must participate during the setting and negotiating of goals to ensure that the proper critical performance variables will be measured. Second, managers must receive periodic updates and exception reports to ensure that there are no surprises, and to measure progress towards goals. Finally, if there are deviations from the standard, management must follow-up or take action (p. 70–71).

A final precaution Simons notes is that there must be strong incentives for motivating individuals to achieve critical performance targets. He suggests that management ensure that it is measuring the correct variables, not making standards too easy, and not selecting goals that are unrealistic (p. 73).

Interactive Control Systems

The purpose of an interactive control system is to provide management with a method for involving themselves regularly and personally in the decision activities of their subordinates. Interactive control systems provide information from sources both internal and external to the organization. Interactive control systems (Table 11) help to focus organizational attention on strategic uncertainties and incite the emergence of new ideas, initiatives and strategies.

Table 11: Interactive Control Systems

What	Control systems that managers use to involve themselves regularly and personally in the decision activities of subordinates
Why	To focus organizational attention on strategic uncertainties and provoke the emergence of new initiatives and strategies
How	By ensuring that data generated by the system becomes an important and recurring agenda in discussions with subordinates
	By ensuring that the system is the focus of regular attention by managers throughout the organization
When	Strategic uncertainties require the search for disruptive change and opportunities
Who	Senior managers actively use the system and assign subjective, effort-based rewards
	Staff groups act as facilitators

There are four defining characteristics of an interactive control system (p. 97). First, information generated by the system must be seen as an important and recurring agenda item addressed by management. Second, the system must demand regular attention by the operating managers within the organization. Third, the data created by the system must be discussed in face-to-face meetings between managers, peers and subordinates. Finally, the system must be a catalyst for the continual challenge and debate of all underlying information, assumptions and action plans.

These four characteristics provide management with the leverage to influence and make the most of the other three systems. By ensuring there is an interactive system, management can reiterate and stress values, vision, codes of conduct or critical performance variables. The interactive system also provides managers the tool to influence experimentation and exploration into potential strategies. Finally, an effective interactive system provides employees with a mechanism for assimilating and sharing organizational learning.

Building on Simons' Model

The model that Simons developed offers managers a holistic context from which to apply specific and general managerial skills and knowledge in a more strategic manner. First, Simons' research has been exclusively aimed at senior management and derives entirely from their point of view. There is little reason to indicate that the model could not be applied to any level of management, or to an individual contributor for that matter. Second, Simons notes that different senior managers focused on one or more of the systems more than others depending on their business strategy. There is, however, no indication of how much time or attention each of the systems required based on the business strategy. It is reasonable to assume that each of the systems may be used more by one level of management than another. For example, we can assume that while a successful first line manager utilizes all four systems, they spend more time and energy in the diagnostic, interactive, and boundary systems, and less in belief systems. Senior management, on the other hand, may spend more time in belief and interactive systems, and less in diagnostic and boundary systems. In essence, where the model depicts each system receiving one-quarter of the 'pie,' the author assumes that the size of the 'piece of pie' may vary depending on one's management level. However, we might also assume that the scope of definition for elements of Simon's model may vary from one level of management to another. A 'business strategy' for a senior manager may include a plan of action and perspective that spans several product lines, a competitive position, and external realities. A first-line manager's strategy may simply involve ensuring their unit activities are closely aligned with those of their manager and closely related work processes. Other elements of Simon's model may be very similar regardless of management level.

Summary of Simons' Model

The ability to focus organizational attention on agendas linked to business strategy is the hallmark of an effective manager (Kotter, cited in Simons, 1995a). Other scholars (Kouzes and Posner, 1993; Olian & Rynes, 1992; McCall & Kaplan, 1990; and Bennis, 1989) have shown that the inability to define vision, focus employee activities and organizational resources, measure and communicate critical success factors are descriptive of poor managers. Several researchers (Robinson and Robinson, 1989; Marsick, 1987) have suggested that skill and knowledge training without a context for applying the skills and knowledge is ineffective. Simons' research and model of belief, boundary, diagnostic and interactive control systems offers managers a holistic context from which to apply specific and general managerial skills and knowledge in a more strategic or transformational manner to enhance both organizational productivity and managerial success on-the-job.

For organizations to enhance their effectiveness, they must continually adapt to a wide variety of unpredictable, rapid, and often erratic environmental conditions such as changes in the workforce, society, competition, technology and organizational structures. Organizations that cannot adapt to these forces will not be able to competently and effectively turn opportunities into valued services and/or products for its customers (Simons, 1995a). Managers serve a critical role as the "specific organ" charged with ensuring that the organization is productive and effective (Drucker, 1986). Simon's research focusing on senior management in ten Fortune 500 companies, indicates that the ability to balance the need for innovation and control to achieve business strategy is a crucial competency for success. His theory suggests these senior managers achieved profitable growth by controlling the tension between creative innovation and the need for predictable goal achievement using the four 'levers,' or 'systems' of control (Simons, 1995a).

SUMMARY OF LITERATURE REVIEW

Contributors to four major models of management including the Rational Goal Model, Internal Process Model, Human Relations Model, Behavioral Model, and Open Systems Model were reviewed in this chapter. Each model was defined and the contributions of each theorist were identified. In this chapter it has been shown how several management models have built upon each other to expand the role managers are expected to fulfill in today's organizations. The chapter concluded with a description of Simons' systems model of management, and the major management roles and practices identified by Simons.

It has been shown that in today's fast-paced, dynamic environment, managers play a critical role in assisting the organization to compete effectively and efficiently (Sayles, 1993). Merely focusing on the traditional roles or planning, organizing, controlling and delegating will not ensure the level of success required.

While the Rational Goal Model of management helped managers become more efficient by focusing on tasks or definitive work assignments, its single-minded focus on improving productivity was seen by many as limiting. Researchers reflective of the Internal Process Model enhanced the Rational Goal Model by describing the various 'managerial functions' that made up the totality of managerial work as they knew it, but failed to consider the human element of the workplace. Adherents of the Human Relations Model built on previous models by adding the element of 'getting things done through others.' Researchers who advocated the Behavioral Model stressed that the study of management must also include worker interpersonal relationships. And finally, the advocates of the Open-Systems Model suggested that managers live in highly unpredictable environments and recognized that managers must be adaptable and flexible in order to succeed. Considered as a whole, these models have attempted to develop and present the tasks, duties, functions and responsibilities of a manager. What each lack individually and together is a defining context which can assist managers to integrate the tasks, duties and responsibilities together in a rational, holistic manner that is tied to the strategic direction of the organization.

For organizations to enhance their effectiveness, they must continually adapt to a wide variety of unpredictable, rapid, and often erratic environmental conditions such as changes in the workforce, society, competition, technology and organizational structures. Simons' research and model of belief, boundary, diagnostic and interactive control systems offers managers a holistic context from which to apply specific and general managerial skills and knowledge in a more strategic or transformational manner to enhance both organizational productivity and managerial success on-the-job.

While Simon's research indicates that excellent senior managers utilized belief, boundary, diagnostic and interactive control systems, he does not indicate the extent or amount of time these managers spent on tasks or activities related to these quadrants. Further, Simons does not indicate if or to what extent middle or first line managers utilize these systems. In the next chapter, the methodology for conducting this research effort is described.

CHAPTER 3
Research Methodology

In this chapter the reasoning behind the selection of the research methodology used to conduct this research will be described along with a description of how the data were collected. This chapter is divided into six sections: Description of the Research Methodology, Description of the Subjects, Description of the Research Setting, Description of the Research Procedures, Effects of the Observer, and Treatment of the Data.

DESCRIPTION OF THE RESEARCH METHODOLOGY

Purpose

Simon's research indicates that excellent senior managers utilize belief, boundary, diagnostic and interactive control systems, but does not indicate the amount of time these managers spent in tasks or activities related to these systems. Further, Simons does not indicate if or to what extent middle or first line managers utilize these systems. The purpose of this research effort was to explore and examine if, and to what extent successful senior, middle and first-line managers in an organization used these same four or similar systems of control to achieve high productivity and innovation in their areas of responsibility. These three levels of management were drawn from the Texas- based manufacturing division of the company. The author would like to stress that Simon's model has not been shared or adopted in any way at the company as a management or leadership model.

Research Questions

To explore if and how successful senior, middle and first line managers in the integrated circuit manufacturing division of the company apply belief, boundary, diagnostic, and interactive control systems or similar systems, the following questions were formulated.

1. What belief systems undergird senior, middle, and first-line managers' strategy in achieving their organizational goals?
2. What boundary systems do senior, middle, and first-line managers invoke through their management strategy in order to remain focused on organizational goals?
3. What interactive control systems do senior, middle, and first-line managers employ to ensure predictable goal achievement?
4. What diagnostic systems do senior, middle, and first-line managers use to monitor and predict quality and productivity?
5. How do senior, middle, and first-line managers use belief systems, boundary systems, interactive control systems, and diagnostic control systems to link to the business strategy of the company?

Research Method

In considering what research method would be most appropriate for this study, the author considered the type of information that would shed light on the research questions. These research questions were designed to gather information relating to how managers attempt to enact a strategy, beliefs, boundaries, diagnostic measures and interactive communications in their work setting. Beliefs, values, communication styles, descriptions of measurement processes and methods for focusing direction through the application of boundaries are not easily quantifiable. However, these concepts and their application do lend themselves readily to a case-study method. For this reason, a qualitative approach was selected.

There were a number of major characteristics of qualitative research that suggest this method well suited for this study. Qualitative research is well suited for its focus on understanding of the deep meaning of a context or situation (Patton, 1990). First, qualitative research takes a holistic perspective and takes place in a natural setting with human researchers as the primary data-gatherers. The intent of this research was to reveal the management philosophies, strategic thought, tactics, to study these selected issues in detail, and to do so in the managers' work environment. The author also hoped to learn how managers align these systems with business strategy. Second, inductive analysis is employed to allow theory to evolve from data collected. Third, social processes that are native to the setting are recognized, and the value of tacit knowledge is recognized. Fourth, sampling is purposive and used to reveal multiple perspectives and realities. The way in which one manager enacts or aligns these four or similar systems might be different in action or conceptualization from other managers. Finally, the research design is flexible and changes as the author interacts with the subjects and the context (Borg & Gall, 1989).

Guba and Lincoln (1985), support this view of qualitative research and identify five axioms as distinguishing characteristics. First, they observe that the goal of qualitative research is to develop insight personal meaning and insight in a phenomenon. Second, qualitative research views all participants and the environment interacting simultaneously. Third, the qualitative method assumes that there are multiple realities instead of a single reality which can be controlled and predicted. Fourth, in the qualitative method, the individual researcher and the participants or situation being studied are inseparable. In other words, the researcher and participants or situation influence each other, as opposed to the qualitative method which assumes that a researcher may stand apart from the participant or situation. Finally, qualitative research does not pretend to be value-free. Rather, qualitative research attempts to identify those values in order to better describe the situation or participants being studied.

A variety of methods are available for obtaining results in a qualitative research include observation, interviews, review of documents, video-tapes, audio-tapes, and even data that has been previously quantified (Ibid). Patton, (1990) also notes that qualitative methods may include data collection from one or more of three sources: (1) in-depth, open-ended interviews; (2) direct observation, and; (3) written documents (p. 10). Interview data may be comprised of quotations regarding experiences, opinions, feelings, expectations, and knowledge. Observational data may include descriptions of individual or group behavior, activities, and actions. Written documents may include records, correspondence, official publications and written responses to questionnaires or surveys.

The case study as a research strategy was selected as it provides the best approach for capturing the complex realities and interactions between systems and people such as the managers upon which this study focuses (Lincoln & Guba, 1985; Merriam, 1988; Stack, 1995). Patton identified the case study as an appropriate research strategy when the intent is "to understand some special people, particular problem, or unique situation in great depth, and where one can identify cases rich in information- rich in the sense that a great deal can be learned from a few exemplars of the phenomenon in question" (1990, p. 54). Yin (1994) notes that the case study is appropriate when a "why" or "how" question is being asked regarding a contemporary set of events in which the researcher has little to no control. This is certainly true of this research as one of the primary research questions of this study deals with discovering how senior, middle, and first-line managers use belief, boundary, diagnostic, and interactive control systems or similar systems to link to the business strategy of the company.

Potential concerns when utilizing case study research strategy include a lack of rigor, weak generalizability, and unreliability (Yin, 1994, p. 33). Yin suggests that lack of rigor can be controlled by taking care to identify and avoid the influence of personal bias, and following specified procedures. The second concern suggests that case study results provide little basis for generalization. Yin notes that both case studies and quantitative experiments are generalizable to theory and not to entire populations or universes. Yin responds to the final concern by suggesting that the reliability of a study can be strengthened by careful documentation and following a carefully laid out plan and strategy for data collection and interpretation (Ibid, p. 37).

DESCRIPTION OF THE SUBJECTS

Traditional research studies select a sample to be representative of a population with the intent that the results will be generalizable to that population. This type of probability sampling is not possible in qualitative research as making statistical generalizations is not a goal. When the goal of a research effort is to discover, understand or gain insight, non-probability sampling methods may be used (Patton, 1990). Patton terms this type of sampling "purposeful," while Goetz and Lecompte (1984) refer to this sampling method as "criterion-based."

Selection Procedures

Participants in this study were drawn from the manufacturing of the company in Texas. While the company has manufacturing divisions located in both Texas and California, due to limits on time and funding for travel, interviews were conducted only with participants in the Austin site. At the time of this research, the manufacturing division was managed by five senior managers represented by a vice president and four directors. Each director was responsible for one plant. While each director was responsible for manufacturing different types of products, all followed the same four basic production processes. Each of these four processes (or modules), photolithography, etch, thin films, and diffusion, is managed by a middle manager. As these processes operate 24 hours a day, seven days a week, each module has four first-line managers. Each of the four shifts necessary to conduct operations is also managed by a first-line manager.

Participants were identified from representatives from senior, middle and first-line management levels. Due to the structure of the division, the pool from which the sample was drawn included:

- Senior management- 5 participants: 1 vice president, 4 directors
- Middle management- 16 middle managers
- First-line management- 64 first-line managers

Organizationally, the first-line managers report to the middle managers, who report to directors, who in turn report to the vice-president of the division. The relationship between these management levels is illustrated in Figure 3.

A stratified random sampling approach was selected as the purpose of this research was to investigate managerial systems use of senior, middle, and first-line managers. This sampling approach provides a number of benefits including ensuring even representation across each management group and anonymity for participants (Stake, 1995; Phillips, 1991). Within each stratified grouping, a sample of at least forty percent were interviewed. Only managers who had served in their managerial position for at least one year were included in the sample.

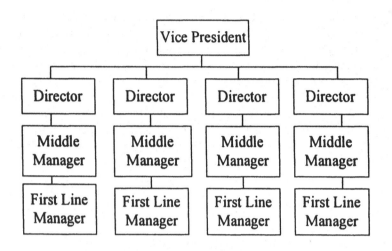

Figure 3: Division Hierarchy

This criterion was selected to ensure that those who participated in the research would have been in the job long enough to have developed some level of comfort, competence and security.

Participants within each stratified grouping were identified through a random sampling selection process. Random selection was accomplished by obtaining an alphabetical list of each stratified grouping and, beginning with the first individual on the list, selecting every fourth individual until the sample size was achieved (Phillips, 1991). From the population of five senior, sixteen middle, and sixty-four first-line managers, this provided a sample of five senior, seven middle, and twenty-six first-line managers for a total of thirty-eight participants. Had it been necessary, this process would have been repeated if any of the individuals selected to participate in the first sample group were not be able to be interviewed due to reasons such as illness, sabbaticals, prohibitive travel schedules, or declining to participate in the study.

DESCRIPTION OF THE RESEARCH PROCEDURES

For the purpose of this research study, three separate categories of data were collected: (1) preliminary data; (2) structured, open-ended interview data; and (3) written documentation data. Each method of data collection is discussed below.

Preliminary Data

First, preliminary data were gathered prior to conducting interviews. The preliminary data consisted of organizational data about the company, the manufacturing division, each plant, and each module within each plant. These data included the overall business strategies of the company, manufacturing division, each plant, and any current information on the nature of the competitive environment characterizing the industry. The purpose of this data was to give the author deeper insight and understanding into the external business environment, and the intended business strategies and activities of the division, each plant, module, and the individuals to be interviewed.

Structured, Open-Ended Interviews

The primary method for collecting data was through the use of structured, open-ended interviews (Patton, 1990). Mishler notes that an interview is "a discourse shaped and organized by asking and answering questions. An interview is a joint product of what interviewees and interviewers talk about together and how they talk with each other" (1986, p. vii). The structured, open-ended interview approach was used as this strategy as the intent of this research was to determine if and to what extent three levels of managers at the company utilized belief, boundary, diagnostic and interactive control systems as identified by Simons. In addition, the interview questions attempted to determine how these three levels of managers identify the qualitative and quantitative elements by which individuals are rated as exceptional achievers, successful achievers, needing improvement or not meeting expectations.

Each participant was interviewed following the same structured list of questions. (For further elaboration, please see Appendix A). By having each respondent answer the same questions, a greater degree of consistency could be maintained. While this method was less flexible and constrained the naturalness of the questions and answers, the structured, open-ended approach allowed the author enough flexibility to focus on the issues which were important to the purpose of the research. In addition, this approach helped to ensure that the author focused on issues which were important to respondents instead of those that may have been important in the researchers mind. The characteristics, strengths and weaknesses of this approach are described in Table 12.

Table 12: Qualities of Standardized, Open-Ended Interview

Characteristics	Strengths	Weaknesses
• The exact working & sequence of questions are determined in advance. • Interviewees are asked the same basic questions in order. • Questions are worded in a completely open-ended format.	• Respondents answer the same questions increasing the ability to compare responses. • Data are complete for each person on topics addressed in the interview. • Interviewer effects & bias are reduced with several interviewers. • Permits users to see instrumentation used in the evaluation. • Facilitates the organization and analysis of data.	• Little flexibility in relating to particular individuals and circumstances. • Standardized wording of questions may constrain and limit naturalness and relevance of questions and answers.

At the outset of the interview, participants were provided with a standard research cover letter (Appendix B) that explained information such as the nature and purpose of the research, that participation in the study was voluntary, that their responses would be kept anonymous, that each question need not be answered, and that the participant could withdraw from the study at any time. All interviews were recorded on audio-tape as there were no participants who objected. In both the cover letter and at the beginning of the interview, the author ensured that each participant was informed of the recording, how the tapes would be used for transcribing purposes, and the procedure for disposing of the tapes.

In addition, the author ensured that each participant was given a copy of a letter of support from the company's Director of Human Resources attesting to the company's support of the research.

Documentation

Third, written documentation was collected from those interviewed such as minutes from staff meetings, monthly and quarterly reports, commendations, letters of appreciation, unit vision, mission and values statements, unit production or quality strategy, and similar materials. Patton (1990) observes that documents "are a basic source of information about program decisions and background, or activities and processes" and "can give the evaluator ideas about important questions to pursue through more direct observation and interviewing" (p. 233).

A major source of documentation the author also collected included copies of performance reviews for the middle and first-line managers. Employees of the company receive an annual review that summarizes performance for the previous year based on several major categories. (For further elaboration, please see Appendix C). These categories include goal achievement for the past year, continuous improvement efforts, teamwork, communications, problem-solving, customer satisfaction, job/company knowledge, and other factors relevant to the job. These ratings are also based on the employee's ability to meet or exceed quantitative goals which may include standards of quality, production and/or defect reduction. Each individual receives a quantitative rating on their annual review that may vary from 'does not meet expectations' (5–10 points), to 'exceptional achievement' (21–24 points). An exceptional rating signals that the individual performed well above what is expected in terms of the quantitative and qualitative indices within each of the major categories listed above on the annual performance review.

The annual performance review data were important for supporting the purposive or criterion-based element of the research. Documentation such as performance reviews have been shown to be helpful in making sense of findings in terms of context (Guba and Lincoln, 1985). The performance review data strengthens this research due to two major criteria. First, performance review data was not easy to obtain. Human Resources maintained these documents in secured employee files. It was only through a strict agreement and process that these data were shared with the author. This process involved having any identifying information in each performance review obscured by a Human Resources employee. Second, the performance reviews were written there by a party other than the interviewer and manager interviewed. Hence, these documents provide a third perspective for triangulating the results of the interviews. By analyzing individual performance reviews, the author was able to compare the preliminary data, interview data, and documentation to minimize threats to validity and reliability.

Additional documentation provided by the Director of Human Resources consisted of the sample group's focal rankings. The company follows a process of ranking each level of management from the 'best' to 'needing most improvement.' This ranking is used to determine pay increases and/or bonus allotment. As with the performance reviews, the focal rankings were provided by the Director of Human Resources so that the identity of each participant could not be determined. The purpose of reviewing these documents was two-fold. First, the author wanted to examine if, and to what extent the performance reviews supported the use and application of Simon's four systems or similar systems. Second, the author wanted to examine the degree of congruence between the qualitative and quantitative criteria each level of management said they valued from their direct reports in terms of exceptional performance, and the actual focal ranking given. Again, the company's Director of Human Resources ensured that these data were provided so that the author was comparing the focal ranking and performance appraisal of each participant without knowing the identity of that participant.

Document review does contain some drawbacks. Some scholars note documents may be incomplete, inaccurate, vary in quality, may not be totally representative, objective, and may pose some problems with validity due to the potential for deliberate deception (Patton, 1990). However, Patton goes on to observe that document analysis is still a valuable adjunct to research as it "provides a behind-the-scenes look at the program that may not be directly observable and about which the interviewer might not ask appropriate questions without the leads provided through the documents" (p. 245).

Engagement with Sample Participants

Once the potential sample participants were identified, they were contacted by the author via telephone to determine their initial interest and commitment in participating in the study. A follow-up letter (Appendix B) was sent to each participant explaining the nature of the study, the interview process, and notifying them that the author would contact them again by telephone to schedule an interview. Interviews were scheduled with each participant in a location that was not distracting and subject to interruptions as few interruptions as possible.

Written Documentation

Participants were asked to provide examples of written documentation that would provide concrete evidence of their success in the job during the past year and the validity of their statements. This documentation included minutes from staff meetings, monthly and quarterly reports, commendations, letters of appreciation, unit vision, mission and values statements, unit production or quality strategy, and similar materials. These materials were analyzed to determine which of Simons systems the tasks or activities described fell, and how the tasks or activities were aligned with the business strategy of the unit and manufacturing division.

EFFECTS OF THE OBSERVER

Any research method requiring an observer is subject to bias on the part of the observer or by effects caused by the presence of an observer on the subjects (Patton, 1990; Denzin and Lincoln 1994). However, these scholars also conclude that these effects can be minimized. This author took a number of steps to safeguard against any threats to the validity of the study. First, it is important to note that this research study was drawn from the manufacturing division within the company, and therefore, the descriptive data are limited in generalizability to other situations. Accordingly, the author is not drawing any conclusions that are ascribed to any setting other than the manufacturing division within the company. Second, it is possible that the research may induce some subjectivity and/or personal bias since the author worked at the company. This close association and familiarity may induce some bias or subjectivity purely because of personal knowledge of the organization, employees, and history. To minimize this bias, the findings were compared and corroborated with the findings between the raw data, findings and observations with participants, and triangulated with documents and observations to ensure objectivity. The author also checked for bias between the interviews conducted by the intern and those by the author. A valid concern when data are collected by more than one individual is the level of subjectivity, data contamination and the loss of confidentiality (Patton, 1990). The training provided the intern addressed issues of subjectivity, the need for accurate recording of participant responses, and the ethical considerations of confidentiality. Beyond that, the author maintained the safety of all audio-tapes and written transcriptions after each interview. The quality of the intern and author interviews were checked by listening to the recordings of the manager interviews while visually reviewing the written transcript. These reviews indicated that there appeared to be no appreciable difference between the manner in which the questions were asked, or by the quality of the transcripts developed by either the intern or author. Finally, participants in this research were drawn from an existing workforce and identified by how well they matched the criteria of 'successful manager.' As this sample of participants does not reflect the general demographic mix of the American workforce or the company, the author is not drawing any conclusions that are ascribed to any setting other than the company's manufacturing division.

TREATMENT OF THE DATA

Data Analysis

Qualitative research relies on data analysis as a method for producing results through a process of analysis, interpretation and presentation of results (Patton, 1990, p. 371). Marshall and Rossman (1989) define data analysis as "the process of bringing order, structure, and meaning to the mass of collected data" (p. 112). They go on to note that in studies of a qualitative nature, both data collection and analysis provide the context for theory that is based on grounded data (p. 113).

Qualitative research also relies on an inductive analysis which is described by Patton (1990) as follows:

> An evaluation approach is inductive to the extent that the researcher attempts to make sense of situations without imposing preexisting

expectations on the phenomenon or setting under study. Inductive
analysis begins with specific observations and builds towards general
patterns. (p. 44)

Inductive analysis allows important dimensions and unexpected themes
to be identified from patterns found in the cases under study.

Analytic Procedure

Strauss and Corbin (1990) and Patton (1990) note that qualitative
research may generate a great deal of data. To deal with the volume of
data collected, the author followed a defined procedure for coding and
making sense of the information A five step process for conducting the
data analysis was followed in this research (Marshall and Rossman,
1989, p. 114– 120).

The first step was to organize the data. This involved reading and
re-reading the data that forces the author to increase familiarity with the
information. Second was a process of generating categories, themes,
and patterns. This process involves reviewing the data and identifying
any notable, grounded categories of meaning that the respondents held.
As the categories, themes, or patterns between the categories become
evident, the author then began the third step by testing emergent
hypotheses. Marshall and Rossman state that this "entails a search
through the data, challenging the hypotheses, searching for negative
instances of the patterns, and incorporating these into larger constructs,
if necessary" (p. 118). The fourth step involved searching for
alternative explanations, or challenging the patterns and themes which
seemed apparent. This involved searching for and finding alternative
explanations for the data and demonstrating how another explanation is
more plausible. The fifth step in the process was to write the report. For
the purposes of this research, writing the report involved presenting the
data gathered through the preliminary analysis, interviews and
document analysis where the respondent views and paradigms are
described.

Validity and Reliability

Guba and Lincoln (1985) note that there is concern that qualitative
research respond to proper standards of trustworthiness. These include:

1. How truthful are the findings of the study and by what criteria can the findings be judged?
2. How applicable are the findings to another setting or group of people?
3. How can we be reasonably sure that the findings would be replicated if the study were conducted with the same participants in the same context?
4. How can we be sure that the findings are reflective of the subjects and the inquiry itself rather than the product of the researchers biases or prejudices?

Guba and Lincoln propose four constructs that reflect the assumptions that underlie qualitative research. These are credibility, transferability, dependability, and confirmability (p. 296). Credibility refers to the ability of the researcher to demonstrate that the research was conducted in a manner that others would feel was accurate and appropriately described. Transferability refers to the ability of the researcher to generalize the findings to other settings or context. Dependability occurs when the researcher attempts to account for changing conditions as well as changes in the design by continually refining and improving the study. Confirmability refers to how objectively the research can be confirmed by another.

Marshall and Rossman go on to state that qualitative research does not pretend to replicable (p. 148). The qualitative researcher must be flexible with design and strategy, hence, other researchers cannot replicate the study exactly. Despite this concern, Marshall and Rossman stress that qualitative research by definition assumes that because reality changes, no study could be exactly replicated. Further, by keeping copious, accurate notes, the researcher allows others to inspect the process followed, and/or analyze the data for themselves.

Several steps have been taken to ensure the reliability and validity of the research analysis. Strauss and Corbin (1990) note that reliability and validity may be obtained in qualitative research by several methods including validating the data against the literature, validating the categories against the data, and having respondents verify the accuracy of the findings. Marshall and Rossman (1989) suggest that validity and reliability can be obtained by following a well designed and implemented analytic process which continually prompts the researcher to reflect critically at distinguishing between reality and the researcher's own perspective or biases.

SUMMARY

In this chapter a review of the methods that were used to conduct this research was presented. A qualitative research method was selected as the most appropriate design for obtaining an in-depth understanding of the way successful senior, middle and first line manager utilize Simons' four systems or similar systems to achieve business strategy. This approach was selected for its focus on the meaning of a context or situation as opposed to a quantitative approach that takes apart a situation to examine its constituent parts, which then become the variables in the research. The case study as a research strategy was selected as it provides the best qualitative approach for capturing complex realities between systems and people such as those that this study encounters. The primary data collection method used consisted of standardized, open-ended interviews. Validity and reliability were supported by checking the results against those of Simons, having respondents check on the accuracy of the findings, and critical reflection throughout the process to distinguish between empirical reality and the researcher's own conceptual perspective.

CHAPTER 4

Results

This chapter is divided into six sections: Review of the Methodology, Demographics of the Sample, Preliminary Organizational Data, Results of Interviews, Performance Data, Analysis, and Summary.

REVIEW OF THE METHODOLOGY

To conduct this research, it was determined that a qualitative research methodology was the most appropriate design for obtaining an in-depth understanding of the way successful senior, middle and first-line managers utilized Simon's four systems or similar systems to achieve their business strategy. Data were collected using three approaches. The first consisted of obtaining preliminary organizational data relating to areas such as business strategy, company values and philosophy of the manufacturing division and each plant. The second, and primary method for collecting data was through structured, open-ended interviews (Patton, 1990). Third, written documentation was collected from participants such as meeting minutes, reports and annual reviews.

DESCRIPTION OF THE RESEARCH SETTING

High tech organizational survival depends on continually and rapidly enhancing employees' skills, knowledge, *while* maintaining high levels of research, design and production. To compete, high tech companies must have cutting edge technology and a workforce that can continuously learn to apply new technologies while delivering the quality and quantity of product customers demand. The vice president for the company's Texas manufacturing division, observed, "Our industry goes through a technological evolution every three to four years. By the year 2000, the skills and knowledge required to support our manufacturing processes will be far beyond what we have today " (cited in Karakakes and McDaniel, 1996, p. 290).

Recognizing this, in 1990 the manufacturing division set out on its Journey To Excellence (JTE) with the directive to "change or go out of business." Senior executives, led by the vice president of manufacturing, met to define a vision and strategy for transforming the company's plant in Texas.

Organizational Profile

In 1969, *Innovation* magazine evaluated the latest semiconductor startup companies and reported that the company's ability to survive was in serious question. On May 1, 1995, the company observed its 26th anniversary. Now the fifth largest US-based manufacturer of integrated circuits, the company is first or second in each of its target markets. Paradoxically, *Innovation* magazine has not been published for 21 years.

There are approximately 13,000 company employees in California, Texas, Japan, Singapore, Malaysia, Thailand, Germany, China, and England. The company has transitioned from making integrated circuit clones to designing and manufacturing world class programmable products and application solutions the company currently partners with IBM, Sony, Fujitsu, Siemens AG, and is a member of SEMATECH, a consortium of US semiconductor manufacturers whose purpose is to maintain America's leadership in semiconductor manufacturing technology.

Industry Profile

One thing is certain about the semiconductor industry's future -- it will be dramatically different from the present. Tomorrow's manufacturers require more advanced tools and skills to make today's dreams a reality. Rogers and Gibson (1991) identify semiconductors and microcomputers as the "highest of high tech" because of the rate technology in these industries is advancing. Other industry leaders include AT&T, Cypress, Digital, Fujitsu, Harris, Hitachi, Intel, Motorola, National Semiconductor, NEC, Texas Instruments, Toshiba, and Samsung.

DEMOGRAPHICS OF THE SAMPLE

The research effort was designed to consist of interviews with five senior managers, seven middle managers and twenty-six first-line managers. Due to production and scheduling requirements, one senior manager was not able to participate in the research. Listed below are the demographics of the sample of senior, middle and first-line managers (Table 13).

Table 13: Sample Demographics

Employee Group	Ethnicity	Gender	Tenure	Total #
Senior Management	American Indian 0 Asian 0 Black 0 Hispanic 0 White 4	Male 4 Female 0	20–25 yrs 0 15–19 yrs 1 10–14 yrs 3 5–9 yrs 0 0–4 yrs 0	4
Middle Management	American Indian 0 Asian 0 Black 0 Hispanic 0 White 7	Male 7 Female 0	20–25 yrs 0 15–19 yrs 3 10–14 yrs 2 5–9 yrs 2 0–4 yrs 0	7
First Line Management	American Indian 1 Asian 0 Black 0 Hispanic 2 White 23	Male 22 Female 4	20–25 yrs 1 15–19 yrs 1 10–14 yrs 4 5–9 yrs 10 0–4 yrs 10	26

The individuals who participated in this research were predominately white males, although there were four females, one American Indian and two Hispanic individuals in the first-line management category. All of the senior managers had a considerable amount of experience in the semiconductor industry and each had been with the company for at least ten years. Among middle managers, all but two individuals had been with the company for at least ten years. As one might expect, those in first- line management positions had been with the company for the least amount of time. Ten first-line managers had been with the company for less than five years and ten less than ten years. Six first-line managers had been with the company for more than ten years.

There was a fairly even distribution of middle and first-line managers represented based on the four major modules (or production processes) within each plant (Table 14). In addition first-line managers represented each of the four modules within each plant. There were two first-line mangers in the 'other' category. These two individuals were, in fact, first line managers and had served in that position in the plant but had moved to a different position shortly before the interview.

Table 14: Plant/Module and Shift Demographics

Employee Group	Plant		Module		Shift	
Senior Management	10 14 15 25	1 1 1 1	Thin films Photo Diffusion- Etch-	n/a n/a n/a n/a	1 A B C D	4 0 0 0 0
Middle Management	10 14 15 25	2 2 3 0	Thin films Photo Diffusion Etch-	1 2 2 2	1 A B C D	7 0 0 0 0
First Line Management	10 14 15 25	8 6 6 6	Thin films Photo Diffusion- Etch Other	5 5 6 8 2	1 A B C D	1 6 8 8 3

Because of their recent knowledge of this position, these two individuals were included in the research. Senior managers are responsible for the operations of all four modules and were marked 'not applicable' in the module block of the table. Both senior and middle managers work only on 'A' shift, which corresponds to a typical eight hour workday. First-line managers work a variety of responsible for the operations of all four modules and were marked 'not applicable' in the module block of the table. Both senior and middle managers work only on 'A' shift, which corresponds to a typical daylight workday. First-line managers work a variety of shifts, with 'A' and 'C' being primarily daylight hours and 'B' and 'D' being primarily night hours.

Seventeen of the first-line managers worked the day shifts while only nine worked evening shifts. This is reflective of the fact that there are more employees on the day shifts than on night shifts at this semiconductor company.

PRELIMINARY ORGANIZATIONAL DATA

To learn more about the company and manufacturing division, information was gathered from a variety of sources including:

- Annual reports
- Published internal interviews with key executives
- Published interviews with key executives in periodicals
- Internal company publications (newsletters, conference summaries, etc.)
- Reports describing the results of internal cultural or organizational change initiatives
- Manufacturing plant operations reviews

Information and data from these sources were collected to provide the author with additional insight into the external business environment, and the values and intended business strategies of the company, manufacturing division, and each plant.

Results of Preliminary Data Analysis

Organizations in the high technology industry are required to continuously improve the performance and quality of their products and services to compete effectively with their competitors. In order to improve products and services at a high rate, the skills and knowledge of employees must be constantly enhanced so that the 'next-wave' of technology can be understood. This company had moved from manufacturing clones of Intel products to offering its own state-of-the-art microprocessors (Rodengen, 1997). The economic pay-off from this successful transition can be inferred from the actual and expected revenues for 1996 and 1997. In 1996, the company reported total revenues of just under $2 billion, while in 1997, the company expected to achieve revenues of $2.5 to $3 billion (Sanders, 1997). This leap in growth does not come easily. The company's senior executives recognized that success was contingent upon enhancing both the company culture and the skills and abilities of its employees (Dialog, 1997).

Preliminary Analysis—Company

The chairman and chief executive officer, espouses a personal approach which stated, "People first, products and profits will follow" (Sanders, 1997, p. 16). A review of the documents and publications from the company provided a great deal of substantiation for the comments. To explore the nature of the preliminary data relating to this organization, the author created a summary of key words or phrases that reflected the business strategy, belief systems, boundary systems, diagnostic systems and interactive control systems of the company as a whole entity. The results of this analysis are described in Appendix D.

Company Business Strategy

A review of presentations made by senior executives, annual reports, Internet data and company publications indicated that the company has set aggressive business objectives for 1997. These included increasing revenues by one-third, achieving new levels of technology, and attracting major new customers (Sanders, 1997). The company's strategies appeared to recognize the major 'drivers' of the high technology business environment including the need to develop products that meet customer needs in terms of cost, cycle time, performance and complexity (Reinertsen, 1997). Further, the strategies recognized the need to partner with others through strategic alliances and joint ventures in order to meet company goals (Sayles, 1993).

Company Beliefs

In order to achieve company goals and strategies, the company had adopted a position that can be viewed as 'people-oriented.' The company's purpose, vision, mission and values (Appendix D) all stress the importance of people (customers and/or employees) as catalysts for success. Success, defined by a purpose statement, translates into exceeding expectations by helping customers 'lead more productive lives' (1996, p.4). Both the vision and mission statements contain elements that stress a 'commitment to values,' 'a culture that brings out the best in each of us,' and leadership in process technology and technology and design (Ibid., p. 6–8). The values statement lists six factors that support the statement 'people are the ultimate source of competitive advantage' (Ibid., p. 10).

Other statements from presentations and company documents stressed additional beliefs that are important. The CEO noted that "Fairness should be everything. My conviction has been that people should be able to go as far in life as their abilities permit them" (Sanders, 1997, p. 1). Additional themes that recur frequently stress the value of community service, the need to continually learn, and the need for leadership and initiative from all employees.

Company Boundaries

The company appeared to have an orderly system of boundaries that defined the limits to opportunity-seeking behavior. The company's mission statement noted that it produces integrated circuits providing programmable products in concert with applications solutions to manufacturers of equipment for personal and networked computation and communication. This statement makes it clear to employees that the company is in the business of making integrated circuits and products that can be programmed to solve the applications needs of its computation and communications customers. The company does not make products that compete with its customer's products. Other boundary limits are set by documents such as the company's Human Resource policies and procedures, World-wide Standards of Business Conduct, contracting and procurement procedures, and planning and budgeting processes.

Diagnostics

The company measured progress towards its goals in a number of ways including all standard business indices such as total revenue, profit and loss, sales, market share, plant capacity, products produced, patents awarded and stock share price. Other measures included accomplishment and progress towards strategic plans, yearly budgets, customer and employee satisfaction.

Company Interactive Controls

To stay abreast of decision-making activities of employees company executives relied on a variety of vehicles for communication including the company publications, breakfasts with senior staff and employees, monthly update videos, and newsletters. Information that is time-sensitive is handled quickly thorough all-employee e-mails or voice-messages. The company stayed current with the external environment through memberships in a number of industry-related organizations such as SEMATECH, the Semiconductor Industry Association, Center for the Study of Work Teams, joint ventures with other companies, review of technical and trade journals and involvement of employees in external educational and conference opportunities. There are also a number of senior and line level internal conferences and cross-functional workgroups that were useful for assisting key management staff to stay involved in the decisions and planning of subordinates. Finally, the company also provided a variety of alternatives for recognizing and rewarding behavior such as bonuses, stock awards, sabbaticals, recognition trips and cash awards.

The company's emphasis on creating a positive workplace was reflected in part by the company being selected as one of the "100 Best Companies to Work for in America" in every edition of the book of the same title by Bob Levering and Milton Moskowitz. In recognizing this award, the company president stated, "During the past two years, we have undertaken a major effort to assure that we 'live our values.' As you know, we have recently adopted several statements that embody our purpose, mission, vision and values--in short, the values and aspirations that define our corporate culture. If each of us will continue to be guided by our values in every aspect of our professional lives, we will truly deserve to be ranked among the best companies to work for in America!" (1997, p. 1).

Preliminary Analysis- Manufacturing Division

Several major 1997 goals dealt specifically with manufacturing and sales of microprocessors. The manufacturing division was tasked with the responsibility for manufacturing the vast majority of products produced by the company. Increasing both the revenue of the company by one-third and achieving increasing levels of technology placed the manufacturing division under heavy scrutiny. To explore the nature of the preliminary data relating to the manufacturing division, the author created a summary of key words or phrases that reflected the business strategy, belief systems, boundary systems, diagnostic systems and interactive control systems of the company as a whole entity. The results of this analysis are described in Appendix E.

Manufacturing Division Business Strategy

A review of internal documents and publications indicates that the manufacturing division has a clear and measurable business plan. The manufacturing division completes a detailed five-year plan that was updated yearly. This confidential company document identified the mission, capabilities goals and strategy needed for the division to achieve its desired outcomes down to the individual plant level. The mission, goals and business strategy was not just provided for the division as a whole, but as an integrated plan for how all plants must work independently and together. Further, the division five-year plan also identified the strategies and results expected from joint-business or venture relationships with other companies.

Manufacturing Division Beliefs

To achieve the mission, goals and objectives described in the five-year plan, the division has developed an initiative, termed the Journey to Excellence (JTE). This effort was begun by senior division executives who recognized that the level of employee skills and workplace hierarchy would have to change if higher levels of productivity were to be achieved. In 1990 the division began the JTE effort with the directive to "change or go out of business" (Karakekes & McDaniel, 1996, p. 290). As a result, a detailed master plan was developed and implemented that places a high premium on quality, customer service, team building communication, alignment, empowerment and advanced human resource practices (JTE, 1995). Integral to this master plan were seven principles that would serve as the context for activities needed to achieve the plan. These principles were to insure customers drive quality, treat everything as a process, improve continuously, build in quality from the start, solve problems using facts and data, involve everyone, and lead through active management.

Manufacturing Division Boundaries

The manufacturing division had an effective system of boundaries that define the limits to opportunity-seeking behavior. In addition to limits detailed in the company documents described earlier, limits were laid out in detail in the manufacturing division's mission statement. Boundaries for behavior were described and reinforced in division and plant documents, videos, presentations and training efforts. Due to the nature of the manufacturing environment, there were clear performance metrics and process specifications that define how work was accomplished. Most recently, the division purchased and was in the process of implementing an automated multi-rater feedback software package that would allow individuals and their managers, peers, co-workers and subordinates to provide feedback on both the quality of their work and how (the manner of behavior) that work gets accomplished. This sent a clear signal that the boundary is not just what one did, but also how one got the job done with relation to others.

Manufacturing Division Diagnostics

Simply put, the division had highly complex measurement systems in place that tracked, measured and reported status on every piece of equipment and every integrated circuit being manufactured. Diagnostic systems were also in place to measure and report progress on what could be termed 'soft' initiatives such as training, human resource practice improvements and cultural changes. A process was defined and implemented within the manufacturing division which was intended to align metric, team and individual goals from the individual level to the plant level. This process, termed, Semi-Annual Goals Achievement (SAGA) began with the senior staff setting the metric goals for major indices within each plan. Each management level below then inputs the metrics required at their level to achieve those above, and so on down to the individual level. As the name 'SAGA' suggests, progress is measured on a semi-annual basis. The results were reported in high level meetings to division executives thereby stressing the importance and visibility of the initiative.

Manufacturing Division Interactive Controls

The manufacturing division developed a number of methods for ensuring that its management were aware of the external environment and the planning and activities of employees. Many of these methods were the same used by the company including company publications, breakfasts with senior staff, monthly update video's and newsletters. Time-sensitive information could be distributed quickly through voice-message, e-mail or pagers. The manufacturing division staff remained informed about the external environment through memberships in industry-related organizations such as SEMATECH, the Semiconductor Industry Association, Center for the Study of Work Teams, joint ventures with other companies, review of technical and trade journals, and involvement of employees in external educational and conference opportunities.

Internally, the manufacturing division also held yearly alignment conferences with all employees to obtain feedback and ensure alignment with organizational objectives. There were also numerous cross-functional workgroups that were useful for assisting key management staff to stay involved in the decisions and planning of subordinates. Senior, middle and first-line manufacturing plant management also met regularly with employees, natural workgroups and problem-solving teams to stay abreast on initiatives.

RESULTS OF THE INTERVIEWS

The second, and primary method for collecting data was through structured, open-ended interviews (Patton, 1990). Interviews were conducted with thirty-seven individuals within the manufacturing division. These included four senior managers, seven middle managers and twenty-six first-line managers. The interview questions were developed to probe if, and to what extent senior, middle and first-line managers in the division apply the systems identified by Simons to achieve high productivity and innovation in their areas of responsibility. All participants were asked to respond to the same 26 questions (Appendix A) following a structured, open-ended approach in order to achieve a higher level of consistency among responses.

Interviews were conducted by the author and a graduate intern from the University of Texas, Department of Educational Administration. The intern spent the first six weeks of employment supporting a separate research effort which involved conducting focus groups with teams of non-exempt workers from the manufacturing areas. This experience was helpful in refining his questioning skills, understanding of the business, and manufacturing environment. The intern also attended 16 hours of training to ensure he understood the terminology and the manufacturing areas, and would be proficient in conducting interviews. This training included:

- An overview of Natural Work Group Teams Skills Training
- An overview of the manufacturing division's Team Empowerment Continuum
- Training in facilitation & interviewing skills

Finally, the author and intern conducted several 'dry-runs' through the interview questions and protocol to ensure both understood the intent of each question, how transitions from topic to topic would be handled, and how to respond to questions or issues raised by the research participants.

Prior to the interview, each participant was provided with a letter from the author describing the nature and purpose of the research, the voluntary nature of the research, anonymity that would be maintained, and notice that the participant could withdraw from the study if desired. Interviews were then scheduled and at the outset of the interview, the author or intern restated this information. In addition, the author or intern noted that the interview would be recorded for transcribing purposes, and that all tapes and written notes would be destroyed at the conclusion of the study.

Coding of Interview Data

Data analysis using qualitative research methods attempted to bring a sense of meaning and order to the volume of interview data obtained (Marshall and Rossman, 1989). The approach taken in this research effort followed an inductive method (Patton, 1990) which began with making general observations and moved to identifying specific patterns or categories.

The first step in the process of coding the interview data was to organize the data into transcripts. These transcripts were read several times to ensure the author became familiar with the content of the interviews. At this time, categories and patterns began to emerge and tables were constructed to aid the author in identifying notable categories of meaning that the respondents held. This latter process led the author to develop a schema for helping identify the extent to which a manager did or did not have a business strategy, the four systems described by Simons, or a method of integrating those systems. Based on an individual's response to a question, the author applied the following criteria to determine the degree of evidence for or against the system:

- Insufficient evidence- based on the response, one could not make any determination for the existence or non-existence of the system.
- Very strong evidence against- based on the response, one could accurately determine that the system did not exist.
- Strong evidence against- based on the response, there was some evidence that the system probably did not exist.
- Some evidence for- based on the response, there was some evidence that the system probably did exist.
- Strong evidence for- based on the response, there was strong evidence that the system did exist.
- Very strong evidence for- based on the response, there was clear evidence that the system existed.

Examples of responses which illustrate these criteria included the following responses to the question, "Do your direct reports have a defined set of values that guide their job performance and interactions with others?":

- Insufficient evidence- There were no instances in which the response could not be assigned to one of the other five criteria.
- Very strong evidence against- "No, that is something we need to do, but we haven't done so yet."
- Strong evidence against- "Well, we all know what values are important, but we have never talked about them or anything."
- Some evidence for- "Yes, two years ago when our team first formed we wrote some values down, but we haven't looked at them for a long time."

- Strong evidence for- "We have developed a written set of values and we revisit them once a year during our alignment session."
- Very strong evidence for- "Oh yeah, of course. These are our values that are posted here (points at framed document). We use a peer review process and a team process to measure how well we live our values twice a year as part of the SAGA process."

As the responses above suggest, some respondents simply stated that they did not have a system in place, while others were able to articulate the system very clearly and demonstrate evidence of that system.

Results of Interviews

The interviews were conducted to determine if, and to what extent senior, middle and first-line managers in the manufacturing division use the four systems or similar systems to achieve high productivity in their areas of responsibility. At the beginning of each interview the author asked two questions to determine what qualitative and quantitative areas senior, middle and first-line managers viewed as indicative of their highest performing direct report and those ready for promotion to the managers level. Two follow-on questions requested information on the areas of improvement most commonly needed by direct reports, and the criteria used to determine if and when a direct report was failing in their job. These four questions served to get the interview off to a start and provide the author with data on the general quantitative and qualitative characteristics or indices the participant viewed as positive or detrimental to success. Twenty-two additional interview questions were intended to determine if and how successful senior, middle and first-line managers in the division applied belief, boundary, diagnostic, and interactive communication systems. These latter twenty-two questions specifically addressed the following research questions:

1. What belief systems undergird senior, middle and first-line managers' strategy in achieving their organizational goals?
2. What boundary systems do senior, middle, and first-line managers invoke through their management strategy in order to remain focused on organizational goals?
3. What interactive control systems do senior, middle, and first-line managers employ to ensure predictable goal achievement?

4. What diagnostic control systems do senior, middle, and first-line managers use to monitor and predict quality and productivity?
5. How do senior, middle, and first-line managers use belief systems, boundary systems, interactive control systems, and diagnostic control systems to link to the business strategy of the company?

To present the responses to the research questions, a summary of the responses was presented by first describing to what degree each management group did or did not have a business strategy, followed by the responses to each research question. Finally a discussion of the trends across all groups were presented along with other observations made during the interviews.

Senior Management Interview Results

Interviews with the four senior managers indicate that all four had Simons' systems in place and that these systems supported the company business strategy (Table 15). The senior manager business strategies were described in detail within the five-year planning guide that identifies the mission, capabilities, goals and strategies needed for the plant to achieve their desired outcomes.

Two of the four senior managers noted that they had developed values statements with the assistance of their direct reports in the past, while two others indicated they were moving towards incorporating the company's values. All four also noted that personal modeling was the most effective means for conveying the importance of values to their direct reports. Further, each senior manager observed that modeling values was not a singular activity, but a behavior to exemplify at all times, "You have to have alignment between what you do and what you say. People are quick to see if what you say you value and how you really behave is in sync." All four of the senior managers stated that they specifically mentioned the 'value of values' several times a year in department meetings or plant alignment sessions.

Table 15: Systems Evidence - Senior Management

Element	Insufficient evidence	Very strong evidence against	Strong evidence against	Some evidence for	Strong evidence for	Very strong evidence for
Business Strategy						4
Belief Systems					2	2
Boundary Systems						4
Diagnostic Systems						4
Interactive Systems					1	3
Alignment				1	1	2

Senior management also appeared to have well defined boundaries that defined their area of responsibilities. In addition to the company boundaries, the division and each plant must comply with ISO 9000 certification requirements. ISO 9000 is an international certification which requires a company to specify what products it makes, the level of quality to which it makes those products, and then document the process by which the organization achieves that level of quality. The result is a continuous improvement effort that was documented by detailed policies and procedures and subject to annual audits. Other processes and activities for boundary management included performance reviews, staff meetings, individual meetings and various reports. There were no data to suggest there was a 'right amount of time' one would spend in boundary management. Only one senior manager indicated they felt they could spend more time in this area. All felt their direct manager and direct reports spent about the right amount of time ensuring boundaries were respected.

The plants had complex systems for monitoring production. Activities senior management noted for monitoring diagnostics included daily, weekly, monthly and quarterly meetings, 1:1 meetings with staff, team meetings and performance reviews. There was no trend in terms of how much time each spent monitoring diagnostics. All four reported that their manager and direct reports did a good job of monitoring diagnostics.

All four senior managers reported involving themselves appropriately in both internal and external activities to influence direction and stay informed. The internal activities included performance reviews, 1:1 meetings, staff meetings and problem-solving teams. External activities included reviewing of professional journals, attendance at industry events, and discussions with vendors. All reported they believed their manager and direct reports spent the right amount of time in interactive control systems. A summary of the responses from senior management regarding their business strategy, belief, boundary, diagnostic and interactive control systems were provided in Table 16.

Table 16: Senior Management Interview Results

Systems	Response Summary
Business Strategy	• Described in detail in 5-year plan
	• Progress to goals reviewed weekly
	• Managers had rapid access to the 5-year plan & supporting documentation
	• All had 'hard' manufacturing business strategies and 'soft' human or organizational strategies
Belief Systems	• All are transitioning to the company values
	• Two also had their own written values statements
	• All reported that primary means of conveying values was through personal role modeling of those values
	• All indicated that conveying values is something one models all of the time (all actions & behavior convey values)
	• All indicated they spent about the right amount of time conveying values
	• All indicated that direct manager did a good job of conveying values
	• Three indicated that their direct reports did a good job of conveying values; one indicated their direct reports could convey values more
Boundary Systems	• Written division and plant performance metrics and reporting processes provide the primary focus for maximizing productivity
	• Activities- performance reviews, 1:1 & staff meetings, & monitoring reports
	• All but one manager indicated that they spent the right amount of time managing boundaries; one indicated that workload and hiring took away time from effective boundary management.
	• There was no common response to percent time spent managing boundaries (varied from 10% to 100%)
	• All felt their direct manager did a good job of boundary management
	• All felt their direct reports did a good job of boundary management

Diagnostic Systems	• All had clear, well-defined diagnostic systems relating to 5–year plan • Activities include daily, weekly, monthly and quarterly reports, staff meetings, 1:1 meetings, & performance reviews • There was no common response to percent time spent monitoring diagnostics (varied from 'all the time' to 15 %) • All felt they spent the right amount of time monitoring diagnostics • All felt their manager spent the right amount of time monitoring diagnostics • All felt direct reports spent the right amount of time monitoring diagnostics
Interactive Control Systems	• All reported involving themselves in internal and external methods for involvement in subordinate planning & decisions • Annual reviews, 1:1 & staff meetings, problem-solving teams, informal interactions, seminars, journal review, discussions with experts in the field • There was no common response to % time spent on interactive controls • All felt they spent the right amount of time on interactive controls • All felt their direct manager spent the right time on interactive controls • All felt direct reports spent the right amount of on interactive controls

Senior managers were also asked how they aligned belief, boundary, diagnostic and interactive control systems with their business strategy. All four of the senior managers responded using language that specified three components- direction, goals and communication of these components to others.

> Having a clear direction and goals is the first step, but you have to understand the big picture, the whole system and how it works so that you can communicate that to your staff.

> I balance these by being results oriented, making and keeping commitments, and making sure everyone knows what the game plan is.

Middle Management Interview Results

Interviews were conducted with seven middle managers suggest that most had some systems in place to help achieve business strategy (Table 17). A major difference between the responses given by middle and senior management was the level of clarity provided. For example, only three of the seven middle managers could put their hands on a document that detailed their business strategy. Four middle managers were able to discuss their strategy in clear terms, but could not readily put their hands on a copy. Another distinction was that only two of the middle manager plans' appeared to have references to human or organizational change strategies; the remainder dealt mostly with the acquisition of new technology and/or meeting unit production goals.

None of the middle managers interviewed had developed a set of written values with their direct reports. Most indicated that they relied on existing values such as those espoused in the Zenger Miller 'Basic Principles' (1997), the division's Journey to Excellence principles, or informal values. One manager responded, "We do have values, and I'm not sure how clearly they are defined, but we all know which values are important." Five of seven middle managers noted that modeling was their primary means of conveying values, while two observed that they conveyed or mentioned values when engaged in activities with their direct reports. Typical activities that allowed all seven managers to covey values were staff meetings, performance reviews, and 1:1

Table 17: Systems Evidence - Middle Management

Element	Insufficient evidence	Very strong evidence against	Strong evidence against	Some evidence for	Strong evidence for	Very strong evidence for
Business Strategy				4	2	1
Belief Systems	1	4		2		
Boundary Systems				1	4	2
Diagnostic Systems					1	6
Interactive Systems				1	5	1
Alignment				4	2	1

meetings with staff. While only four of seven middle managers noted that they spent 100% of their time modeling values, all stressed the importance of values. One individual noted, "There are no simple answers to 'how much time do I spend on values. It's all the time. Everything you do must fit into the big picture and how you behave towards others is a major part of the picture." Others noted the importance of showing that even they make mistakes,

> I think it's important to let people see that when you make mistakes you immediately correct them according the values you believe in. For example, once I was in a meeting and I snapped at one of my engineers for something they had done in good faith, but had not gone well. I could see the reaction on everyone's face, including hers, and stopped right then to apologize and make it clear that what I did was not acceptable behavior.

Roughly the same percentage of middle managers felt they spent about the right amount of time conveying values as senior managers indicated. (Three senior managers indicated that they felt their direct reports spent about the right amount of time on values compared to five of seven middle managers.) Five of seven middle managers also felt their manager and direct reports spent the right amount of time conveying values.

All seven middle managers had elaborate systems for monitoring progress towards unit production goals. As with senior management, common activities included performance reviews, monitoring reports, staff meetings, team progress reviews, problem-solving reviews and 1:1 meetings with staff. Common responses in this category noted how important 'getting results' was to success. All reported that they spent the right amount of time monitoring boundaries although the amount of time spent ranged from 5% - 60% with an average of 30%. Six of seven noted that their managers spent the right amount of time monitoring boundaries. One noted, "My manager is way too focused on tactical work and has never once asked me about the direction I've set for my area or the method I plan to use to get there." Three of seven middle managers stated that they felt their direct reports appropriately monitored boundaries, while four observed that they felt their direct reports could improve in this area. A frequent observation by middle managers was that the first-line managers had a large workload which forced them to focus on very 'day-to-day' tactical issues.

All middle managers had clearly defined and comprehensive diagnostic systems for monitoring progress towards unit goals. Typical activities included performance reviews, staff meetings and monitoring reports. All reported that both they and their managers spent the right amount of time monitoring diagnostics. Only one noted that their direct reports could spend more time on diagnostics. This manager observed, "My direct reports aren't sure where they are going. They are measuring things, but it's mostly day-to-day management. I am trying to help them see how to use measurement to look long-term."

All seven middle managers reported that they were well involved interactively with their direct reports. Activities common for this area included performance reviews, 1:1 staff meetings, regular staff and problem-solving meetings, team reviews and passdowns. They also reported spending time reviewing professional journals, attending workshops or conferences, and discussions with other engineers. All but one felt they spent the right amount of time on interactive controls. Six of seven indicated both their manager and direct reports spent the right amount of time on interactive controls.

A summary of responses given by middle managers with regard to their business strategy, belief, boundary, are provided in Table 18. Five of the seven middle managers gave responses that mirrored those from senior management with regard to how they integrated the four systems:

We use the Semi-Annual Goal Achievement indices to align the unit. I try to take the big picture of the division and see what direction we are headed and try to align the division, unit and team goals so that everyone is supporting each other and we are all focused on the right things.

The alignment process drives the division and unit goals right on down to each individual's goals. They all need to be aligned and understand how the all fit in and support each other.

Table 18: Middle Management Interview Results

Systems	Response Summary
Business Strategy	• 5 of 7 middle managers had written business strategy; 2 had metric indices tied to unit goals • Only 2 had rapid access to the business strategy • Only 2 had strategies that incorporated 'soft' human or organizational strategies in addition to metric or technology.
Belief Systems	• 0 middle managers had developed values with their employees; all reported using Zenger Miller principles, JTE or informal values • 5 of 7 conveyed values through modeling, 2 of 7 through activities • Common activities included QGA's, staff meetings, 1:1's • 4 of 7 indicated 100%; 2 of 7 indicated 10– 20%; 1– no idea • 5 of 7 indicated that they spent the right amount of time conveying values; 2 indicated they could spend more 5 of 7 indicted their manager spends the right amount of time • 5 of 7 indicated their direct reports spend the right amount of time
Boundary Systems	• All had monitoring systems for focusing on unit production goals • Common methods for ensuring boundaries were QGA's, project plans, daily, weekly & monthly reports, team progress reviews, 1:1's, staff meetings, passdown meetings • Time spend in boundary management ranged from 5% to 60% with the average being 30% • All reported that spend the right time monitoring boundaries • 6 of 7 indicated their manager spend the right amount of time monitoring boundaries • 3 of 7 stated their reports maintained the right amount of time managing boundaries; 4 of 7 indicated this was not the case

Diagnostic Systems	• All had diagnostic systems to ensure progress towards unit goals • Common activities were QGA's, production metrics, staff meetings • All reported spending the right time monitoring diagnostics • All reported their manager spent the right amount of time monitoring diagnostics • 6 of 7 reported that their reports spent the right amount of time monitoring diagnostics
Interactive Control Systems	• All reported involvement in the activities and planning of reports • Activities were performance reviews, 1:1 & staff meetings, problem-solving meetings, team reviews, passdown, seminars, conferences, meetings with vendors • 6 of 7 indicated spending the right amount of time • 6 of 7 indicated their manager spend the right amount of time; 1 indicated this was not the case • 6 of 7 indicated their direct reports spent the right amount of time; 1 indicated this was not the case

We build a positive environment that reinforces the entire value system. The values lay the foundation for the work environment. We achieve direction by involving different people so they know where we are, and communicate the direction so that those in the decision-making processes can respond accordingly. The metrics are somewhat repetitive, so they are ingrained into everyone's thought processes.

Common language included the need to understand the larger picture and purpose of the division, the need to align strategy and goals, the need to communicate with all levels of the organization, and to create a supportive environment based on values. While 'getting results' was not stated explicitly, it was inferred as important given the comprehensive boundary and diagnostic systems middle managers had in place.

First-Line Management Interview Results

Twenty-six first-line managers were interviewed to determine how they used Simon's or similar systems for achieving high productivity (Table 19). There were three trends in the responses of the first-line managers that appear to be different from those of senior and middle management. First, first-line managers were not as positive in their evaluation of the time that they, their manager or direct reports spent in any one system. Second, both senior and middle managers had systems in place that encompassed both the work itself (quantity and quality of work), and how the work was to be accomplished with others whereas first-line managers generally did not feel this way. Third, first-line manager interviews suggested a much more tactical, short-term focus regarding the work they accomplish.

Nineteen first-line managers were able to articulate or show evidence of a business strategy that supported that appeared to support that of the company. These strategies, however, consisted primarily of achieving the metric goals defined on their semi-annual goal achievement form. When asked about strategy, a number of first-line managers simply stated, "My strategy is to meet today's numbers," or "To meet the numbers for this week/quarter" suggesting a tactical focus as opposed to a thoughtful strategy as defined by Simons (1995, p. 8).

Table 19: Systems Evidence - First-Line Management

Element	Insufficient evidence	Very strong evidence against	Strong evidence against	Some evidence for	Strong evidence for	Very strong evidence for
Business Strategy		2	5	8	11	3
Belief Systems		1	9	10	3	3
Boundary Systems				6	17	3
Diagnostic Systems				4	17	5
Interactive Systems				10	15	1
Alignment			6	14	5	1

Two indicated that their business strategy consisted of hiring the right staff, three indicated team development, and two indicated they had no strategy at all.

Of the twenty-six interviewed, only eight mentioned team or individual development as a strategy and none mentioned organizational change. Only six of the twenty-six first-line managers could readily show a copy of their values to the author. Most indicated that they had developed or identified a set of values in the past, but had not revisited them in quite some time. One manager response was typical of this group when he observed, "When the team first formed we developed some values, but we have not gone back and looked at them for some time." Twenty-one first-line managers indicated that they did not have a defined set of values for their workgroups, but rather, relied on ground rules, or a charter or mission statement. The activities the first-line managers employed to convey values consisted primarily of setting an example at team meetings and 1:1 performance reviews. There was no trend for the amount of time first-line managers spent conveying values as the percentages ranged from five percent to one hundred percent. Most first-line managers (seventeen) indicated the time they spent conveying values was the right amount of time while nine indicated they felt they could spend more time in this area. This was slightly lower than what middle managers indicated (65% for first line managers compared to 71% for middle managers). This was also true for first-line managers perception that their manager spent about the right amount of time conveying values. Sixteen indicated that their manager spent the right amount of time conveying beliefs while ten indicated their manager either did not convey any values, or spent very little time in this area. First-line managers working night shifts noted that getting time with their middle manager was difficult to obtain and might account for this trend. A major difference developed between what first line and middle managers reported regarding direct report conveyance of values. Only seven or 27% of first-line managers indicated that they felt their team members spent the right amount of time conveying their beliefs, whereas five or 71% of middle managers felt that first line manager direct reports spent about the right amount of time conveying values. First-line managers that responded that their teams did not spend much time on values observed that they did not really know. One fairly representative response was, "I'd be really surprised if anyone ever brings up the subject of values when I am not around. My impression is that this is just not something they do- they are afraid of looking silly if they 'share their values' with everyone else."

All of the first-line managers indicated that they had some type of system in place to monitor boundaries, although six individuals were not able to articulate the boundaries. Typically boundaries took the form of the processes and procedures for monitoring manufacturing operations. Activities for conducting and monitoring boundaries consisted of attending team meetings, performance reviews and passdowns. Of the twenty-six managers, seventeen spent less than twenty percent of their time monitoring boundaries, two reported between thirty and forty percent, four indicated between forty and fifty and three reported more than seventy percent. First-line managers reported that they spent the right amount of time monitoring boundaries. Another major gap in perception occurred when only nineteen or 73% of first-line managers stated their manager spent the right amount of time monitoring boundaries compared to middle manager assertions that they all monitored boundaries appropriately. Eighteen or 69% of first-line managers indicated that their team members spend the right amount of time monitoring boundaries compared to 6 or 85% from middle managers.

All twenty-six first-line managers had some system for monitoring diagnostics. This appeared to be the strongest and most comprehensive system in operation that tied directly to any business strategy. As with middle managers, the first-line managers spent a good deal of time in meetings, monitoring reports and passdowns to determine metrics. Twenty of the managers observed that they spent enough time monitoring diagnostics, with several of these noting that they probably spent too much time in this area. Twenty-one managers noted that they felt their direct reports also spent about the right amount of time monitoring diagnostics. These responses differed somewhat from middle manager perceptions with six noted that the first-line manager direct reports did spend the right amount of time monitoring diagnostics.

While all twenty-six reported involving themselves in the decisions and planning activities of their subordinates through staff meetings, 1:1 meetings, performance reviews and passdowns, first line manager perceptions differed in each category from those of middle management. Ten of the first-line managers simply noted that they 'attended meetings' but did not clearly articulate how they influenced decision-making of subordinates. Only fifteen first-line managers (58%) felt they spent the right amount of time interactively compared to 85% of middle managers felt. Similarly, twenty first-line managers (76%) reported that their manager spent about the right amount of time interactively compared to 85% of middle managers. Finally, only sixteen first-line managers felt their team members spent the right amount of time interactively compared to 85% for middle managers.

A summary of the responses given by first-line managers with regard to their business strategy, belief, boundary, diagnostic and interactive control systems are described in Table 20.

First line managers gave a variety of responses regarding how they integrated beliefs, boundary, diagnostic and interactive control systems to achieve their business plan. Of the responses, only six first line managers appeared to have a good conceptual idea of how to integrate these systems. Fourteen noted that coordinating activities so that their SAGA goals would be met was one strategy for achieving this balance. One individual used the metaphor of a baseball team, "My team talks about work from the view of a baseball team. We are all on the same team, play the same game, have the same goals and need to understand how our position supports all the others." However, six of the twenty-six front-line managers indicated that they had not given the importance of integrating these systems much thought. Responses that support this observation include the following:

I never really thought of that before, but how you treat people is important.

I'm not sure how I combine them all together, not deliberately.

I don't know if I consciously marry them together.

These responses and those of other first line managers suggested that their primary focus was on meeting tactical, short-term measures of productivity. The differences between perceptions of first-line managers and middle managers might suggest that they do not communicate or share strategies, values, and other elements of their jobs as much as they should. As a result, or as a consequence of this short-term focus, first-line manager strategy may consist primarily of communicating and monitoring metrics in daily to weekly time frames. Other levels of communication such as interpersonal issues, appreciative inquiry, and developmental issues do not appear to be in effect on a wide-spread basis.

OTHER TRENDS

Each interview began with the author asking two initial questions to determine what qualitative and quantitative areas senior, middle and first-line managers viewed as descriptive of their highest performing direct report and those ready for promotion to the next highest management level. Two follow-on questions requested information on the areas of improvement most commonly needed by direct reports, and the criteria used to determine if and when a direct report was failing in their job. These four questions served to establish some level of rapport and provide the author with some data on the general quantitative and qualitative characteristics or indices the participant viewed as positive or detrimental to success.

The author reviewed the responses to these four questions to identify any themes or patterns. Responses to these four questions formed four general categories. These were 1) the ability to set direction and lead, 2) the ability to get results, 3) the ability to establish a supportive environment, and 4) technical skills. Collectively, those interviewed described the ability to set direction and lead others as the ability to 'see the big picture,' to motivate and to articulate a vision. Getting results consisted of one's willingness to take initiative and be accountable for a problem until resolved, and to ensure that the highest leverage goals received the greatest focus. Creating a supportive environment was described as the ability to develop the trust & respect of others, to keep commitments, apply good people skills, team skills, and to be seen as a role model. The final area, technical skills, was described as one's ability to understand and resolve technical problems that occur in the manufacturing environment. In order to make meaning of the responses, the author counted the number of times individuals within each management level stated or described a word or concept that fell into one of the four categories.

Table 20: First Line Management Interview Results

Systems	Response Summary
Business Strategy	• 17 of 26 indicated their primary business strategy consisted of meeting SAGA goals; 3 indicated the strategy was hiring, 4 indicated team development and 2 reported they had no strategy.
	• 8 of 26 mentioned team or individual development as a part of their business strategy
Belief Systems	• 12 of 26 indicated they developed written values with teams, however 4 of these 12 indicated the values had not been revisited since developed; 14 indicated they did not have a defined set of values
	• Activities for conveying values consisted primarily of NWG meetings, 1:1 meetings, performance reviews and passdowns
	• 14 of 26 indicated they spent less than 10% of their time conveying values; 3 indicated 20–25%; 2 indicated 50–60 % and 4 said 100&
	• 17 indicated they spent the right amount of time on values while 9 indicated they did not
	• 16 indicated their manager did spend the right amount of time on values while 10 indicated their manager did not
	• 7 indicated their NWG's spent the right amount of time on values while 19 indicated that the NWG's did not
Boundary Systems	• All 26 managers indicated that they had some system for monitoring unit metrics; only 2 indicated the had team development boundaries
	• Primary activities for boundary management were NWG meetings and monitoring SAGA goals
	• 8 managers said they spent 0–10% monitoring boundaries, 9 indicated 11–20%, 2 said 30–40%, 4 indicated 41–50% and 3 >70%
	• 19 managers indicated that their manager spent the right amount of time monitoring boundaries while 6 did not
	• 18 managers indicated their NWG members spent the right amount of time monitoring boundaries, 8 did not

Diagnostic Systems	• All 26 managers had some system for monitoring diagnostics
	• Primary activities were written reports, daily, weekly & monthly meetings and passdown
	• 20 managers indicated that they spend enough or too much time monitoring diagnostics, 6 indicated they could spend
	• 21 managers indicated their manager spent the right amount of time monitoring diagnostics, 5 indicated they did not
	• 19 indicated their direct reports spent the right amount of time monitoring metrics, 6 did not
Interactive Control Systems	• All 26 said they involved themselves in decisions and planning activities
	• Typical activities included NWG meetings, 1:1 reviews, passdown
	• 15 said they spent the right amount of time interactively, 11 did not
	• 20 felt their manager spent the right amount of time; 6 did not
	• 16 felt their NWG members spent the right amount of time, 10 did not

Best Direct Report

The first question required that managers consider the qualitative and
quantitative areas senior, middle and first-line managers viewed as
indicative of their highest performing direct report. All senior and
middle managers indicated that their best direct report consistently met
or exceeded the quantitative indices established for their area of
responsibility. These are indices that denote production numbers such
as scrap, product quality, and line yield. These indices vary
considerably between both plants and modules within each plant due to
the type of integrated circuit being designed and the maturity of the
plant. For example, a plant producing a product that has been well
established in the marketplace for years can expect much higher indices
than a new, cutting edge product in which the manufacturing process is
still being perfected. First-line managers rarely mentioned exceeding
goals as an important quality of a direct report. Senior and middle
managers identified 'setting direction' as an important quality of their
best direct report, whereas only fourteen first-line managers (54%)
made this observation (Table 21). All first-line, middle and senior
managers observed that 'getting results' was characteristic of their best
direct report. In the area of 'creating a

Table 21: Qualities of Best Direct Report

	Senior Management	Middle Management	First-Line Management
Sets Direction	4	7	14
Gets Results	4	7	26
Environment	4	5	8
Technical Skill	1	0	10

supportive environment,' all senior managers, five middle managers
(71%) and only eight first-line managers (31%) identified this area as
characteristic of their best direct report. In the area of technical skills,
ten first line managers noted that this quality was characteristic of their
best direct report whereas only one senior and no middle managers
made this observation.

Promotional Criteria

Managers were asked to consider what qualitative and quantitative areas senior, middle and first-line managers would view as a requirement to be promoted to the next management level. As with the criteria for best report, all senior and middle managers indicated that their best direct report met or exceeded the quantitative indices established for their area of responsibility (Table 22). First-line managers cited technical skills and the ability to 'meet the numbers' as the major requirements for a promotion to their level. Three senior and all seven middle managers observed that 'setting direction' as consideration for promotion to their level compared to only two first-line managers. For 'getting results,' two senior, seven middle, and sixteen first-line managers identified this quality as important for promotion.

Table 22: Promotional Criteria

	Senior Management	Middle Management	First-Line Management
Sets Direction	3	7	2
Gets Results	3	7	20
Environment	3	4	15
Technical Skill	1	2	24

Three senior managers four middle managers and fifteen first-line managers observed that 'creating a supportive environment' was important for promotion. Similarly, only one senior manager, two middle managers and twenty-four first-line managers noted that technical skills was important for promotion to their level.

Area for Improvement

In order to answer the third question managers had to consider the qualitative and quantitative areas in which managers at their same level needed the greatest improvement. Senior, middle, and first-line managers noted that individuals who needed the most improvement in quantitative terms were those who were having a hard time meeting their production indices. As indicated in Table 23, three senior, five middle and only 1 first-line manager felt that the ability to 'set direction,' was a major area of improvement for individuals

Table 23: Areas of Improvement

	Senior Management	Middle Management	First-Line Management
Sets Direction	3	5	1
Gets Results	1	6	15
Environment	2	4	15
Technical Skill	0	0	6

at their same management level. Only one senior manager, six middle managers and fifteen first-line managers observed that 'getting results' was an area of improvement needed by individuals in their same management level. Two senior, four middle and fifteen first-line managers stated that 'creating a supportive environment' was an important area of improvement needed. Only six first-line managers observed that improving technical skills was an issue within their management level.

Cause for Failure

The final question asked each manager to consider what qualitative and quantitative indicators managers at their same level most frequently lacked which ultimately led to failure in that position. As indicated in Table 24, three senior, seven middle and eight first-line managers felt that the inability to 'set direction' was a primary cause for failure by others in

Table 24: Causes for Failure

	Senior Management	Middle Management	First-Line Management
Sets Direction	3	7	8
Gets Results	2	7	16
Environment	2	4	6
Technical Skill	0	1	16

the same management level. Two senior, all seven middle and sixteen first-line managers observed that the failure to 'get results' was a primary cause for failure by others in the same management level. Only two senior, four middle and six first-line managers noted that the inability to 'create a supportive environment' was a primary cause for failure by others in the same management level. Finally, only one middle manager, and sixteen first-line managers observed that the lack of technical skills was a primary cause for failure by others in the same management level.

The responses from managers regarding the qualities of their best direct report, promotional criteria, typical areas for improvement and causes for failure suggested strong differences between senior, middle and first-line managers. Senior and middle managers placed a higher value on one's ability to set direction, get results and create a supportive environment than did first-line managers. Senior and middle management placed less value on technical skill, where first-line managers clearly felt this was a very important factor. There are a number of possible explanations for these differences. It may be that 'direction' from a first-line manager perspective, is already set. In other words, it would appear that the metrics (or direction) may be given to first-line managers; and not developed at their level. Given the level of focus on 'making the numbers,' and highly technical nature of the manufacturing environment, this result did not appear to be too surprising. Second, three internal organizational analysis indicated that the performance evaluation and reward system are geared towards rewarding results, not developing a supportive environment (Abrams & Elwood, 1995; McDaniel, 1993; McDaniel & Rollins, 1993). However, these same internal assessments observed that progress is being made on this front. Third, as in many work environments, first-line managers were often promoted due to their technical expertise alone- not necessarily their ability to develop others. Thus, it would not be surprising that new managers still rely heavily on and value their technical expertise since they much closer to the shop floor. Senior and middle managers are already 'proven' in technical skill by the time they are promoted and consequently, did not perceive this skill as critical.

PERFORMANCE DATA

The interviews provided data which suggest how each level of management identified the qualitative and quantitative elements by which individuals were rated as exceptional achievers, successful achievers, needing improvement, or not meeting expectations. Interview data were also used to ascertain the degree to which the managers used Simons' four systems or similar systems to achieve high productivity in their area of responsibility. The next step was to determine the correlation between 1) what managers said was important criteria for being rated exceptional, 2) the manager's utilization of Simon's four systems or similar systems, 3) the manager's individual performance appraisal, and 4) their actual focal ranking. Due to the sensitivity of executive performance information, the author was not able to obtain performance appraisals or focal rankings on the four senior managers. However, anecdotal information provided by the human resources director indicated that all four of these individuals were rated equally on both performance reviews and focal rankings. The required data were obtained for the middle and first-line managers and the information below refers to these two latter groups.

Employees of this semiconductor company receive an annual performance review which summarizes their performance for the previous year based on several categories including goal achievement, continuous improvement efforts, teamwork, communications, problem-solving, customer satisfaction, job/company knowledge, and other factors that may be relevant to the job. These ratings are also based on the employee's ability to meet or exceed quantitative goals that may include production indices such as product quality, scrap, yield, equipment utilization and/or defect reduction. Each individual receives a quantitative rating on their annual review that may vary from 'does not meet expectations' (5–10 points), to 'exceptional achievement' (21–24 points). An exceptional rating signals that the individual performed well above what is expected in terms of the quantitative and qualitative indices within each of the major categories listed above on the annual performance review. At the end of each annual review cycle, the sixteen middle managers and sixty-four first-line managers are assigned a 'focal ranking' which numerically ranks each manager from the most outstanding performer to the individual needing the most improvement. Thus, a manager with a focal ranking of 1, was higher on the scale of performance than the manager who received a focal ranking of 16. Raises and bonuses are allotted based on one's focal ranking.

In order to compare the interview results with the sample group performance data, the author obtained copies of performance appraisals and focal rankings. These documents were edited by the Director of Human Resources to ensure confidentiality of each participant. There were two reasons for reviewing these documents. First, the author wanted to examine if, and to what extent the language used in the performance reviews supported the use and application of Simon's four systems or similar systems. Second, the author wanted to examine the degree of congruence between the qualitative and quantitative criteria each level of management said they valued from their direct reports in terms of exceptional performance, and the actual focal ranking given.

The performance reviews were studied and statements or quantitative data relating to the individual's strengths, accomplishments and improvement needs were noted. Once these data were developed, the Director of Human Resources matched the names of the individuals with the identification code given to each participant by the author. This allowed the author to match the individual to their interview data, annual achievement score and focal ranking, and make comparisons across each of these items.

Results of Performance Data Analysis

In order to assess the degree of congruence between what senior, middle and first-line managers said were important qualitative and quantitative qualities, the author examined the language used in each performance review. In doing so, the author attempted to discover if the language used suggested to what extent the individual exceeded, met or fell below the qualitative and quantitative standards identified in the interviews as indicative of high performance. Second, the author attempted to discover if the language used in the performance review suggested to what extent the individual had elements of the four systems identified by Simons. The results of this analysis were then compared to the results of the author's previous interviews with each senior, middle and first-line managers and the rating indicating the degree each utilized Simons four systems or similar systems. The author developed a 'systems average' (Appendix F) suggesting the degree a manager had elements of a business strategy, Simons systems, and the degree to which those systems were aligned with each other and the business strategy. The systems average is the arithmetic average of the business strategy, each of the four systems, and how well the systems were aligned.

To accomplish the next step in the process, the human resources manager then provided the information on each manager's annual achievement score and actual focal ranking. This provided the author with one variable that was nominal (systems average) and two that were ordinal (annual achievement and focal ranking). When selecting statistical techniques for analyzing data in which one variable is ordinal and one nominal, and the ordinal variable is dependent, nonparametric tests are recommended (Blalock, 1972). Nonparametric tests are those "which refer to tests which do not require the normality assumption or any assumption that specifies the exact form of the population" (p. 243) Blalock and others (Snedecor & Cochran, 1989; Moore & McCabe, 1993) also observe that nonparametric tests make some assumptions about the nature of the population, but that these assumptions are generally weaker and less restrictive than those required in parametric tests. Nonparametric tests are justified when "the sample is small and normality cannot be assumed" (Blalock, 1972, p. 244). When the variables being tested cannot be assumed to be normal, the best procedure is to convert the variables to rankings (Snedecor & Cochran, 1989.) Wagner observes that the Spearman rank of correlation coefficient is suitable for "determining if two variables are related, and if so, to what degree" (1992, p. 345).

The procedure the author followed was to list the middle managers, their systems average, annual performance ranking and focal ranking (Table 25). Using a statistical package (SAS/JMP Version 3.2, 1997), the author computed scatter plots for each of the variables (Appendix G).

Table 25: Middle Manager Rankings

Mid-Manager Code	Systems Average	Annual Review	Focal Ranking
V2	4.67	22	3
W2	4.00	21	5
Z2	4.67	21	2
A3	5.67	21	4
B3	5.00	22.6	1
C3	4.50	19.9	7
D3	4.50	20.2	6

Scatter plots are useful for displaying the relationships between two quantitative variables graphically (Moore & McCabe, 1993). By looking at the shape and slope of the scatter plots one may begin to suggest the type of relationship between the variables. The third step in the process was to compute a Spearman Rho correlation of coefficient on the data to determine to what extent each of the variables were related. These results are described in Table 26.

Table 26: Middle Manager Correlation Coefficients

Variable 1	Variable 2	Spearman Rho
Annual	Systems Average	0.55
Focal	Systems Average	-0.66
Focal	Annual	-0.89*

$*p > .05$

As the data indicate, there was a moderate relationship between the annual review and systems average (0.55) and focal review and systems average (0.66) for middle managers. There was a very strong relationship between annual review and focal ranking (0.89) which was statistically significant ($p > .05$) . However, this was a small sample of only seven individuals, therefore, it is difficult to generalize too much from these findings.

The process of listing the data (Table 27), running scatterplots and computing a Spearman correlation of coefficient, was repeated for first-line managers. The scatter plots that were computed along with a outlier analysis which displays the Mahalanobis distance of each point from a multivariate mean. The JMP Statistics and Graphics guide observes that the "standard Mahalanobis distance depends of the estimates of the mean, standard deviation and correlation of the data" (p. 313). The Statistics and Graphics guide goes on to note that "when data are correlated it is possible for a point to be unremarkable when seen along one or two axis, but still be an outlier by violating the correlation. This analysis resulted in the identification of one outlier within the data. This data point was omitted from the computation of the Spearman correlation of coefficient as outliers "usually indicate a problem with the data either through an incorrect measure or a data point that has become different than the others" (Wagner, 1992, p. 76). In the case of the outlier, the subject had a high annual review score (22) and focal rankings (3), but only a moderate systems average (4.5).

Table 27: First Line Manager Rankings

1st Line Mgr. Code	Systems Average	Annual Review	Focal Ranking
I1	4.83	22.5	1
S1	5.17	22.7	2
D2	4.50	22.0	3
H4	4.50	21.5	4
W1	5.50	20.7	5
O2	4.50	21.0	6
T1	4.17	21.4	7
B1	4.50	20.0	8
H2	4.00	20.0	9
X1	5.00	22.6	10
F2	4.33	21.1	11
B2	4.33	21.7	12
J2	4.67	19.5	13
U1	4.83	20.0	14
I2	5.50	19.2	15
A1	4.67	20.2	16
M2	4.50	20.0	17
G2	4.33	20.2	18
E1	4.33	10.9	19
P1	4.67	20.4	20
S2	4.50	18.0	21
M1	3.33	19.7	22
N2	3.83	21.0	23
V1	4.00	21.0	24
T2	3.67	19.0	25
Z1	3.50	19.6	26

The data in Table 28 suggest that there was a moderate relationship between a first-line manager's annual achievement score and systems average. There was a slightly stronger relationship between focal ranking and systems average, and between focal ranking and annual achievement.

Table 28: First-Line Manager Correlation Coefficients

Variable 1	Variable 2	Spearman Rho
Annual	Systems Average	0.45*
Focal	Systems Average	-0.59**
Focal	Annual	-0.66**

$* p > .05 ** p > .001$

The Spearman correlation of coefficient analysis on middle and first line managers appears to suggest that there was some evidence that individuals who had a higher ability to utilize Simon's four systems are also rated higher on annual achievement and focal ranking. Both middle and first-line managers had moderate correlation's between systems average, annual achievement and focal ranking. The relationship between annual achievement and focal ranking in middle managers was very strong, and moderately strong for first-line managers. The stronger correlation between annual achievement and focal ranking in middle managers might be explained by a number of factors. First, the number of individual evaluators in the middle and first-line manager groups varied greatly. The more evaluators, the less consistency one would expect to see. Only one very senior manager rated the other four senior managers. The four senior managers however, in turn rated sixteen middle managers, who were responsible for rating sixty-four first-line managers. A second influencing factor for middle managers is that all were ranked fairly high, with a range on their annual reviews of only 2.7 points from 19.9 to 22.6. The annual review average for the middle manager group was 21.1. For first-line managers, the annual performance review range was a broader at 4.7; from 18 to 22.7. The annual achievement review average of 20.6 for this group was slightly lower than for middle managers. A third factor that may have influenced the outcomes could be the speaking skill or mental state of the manager when he/she was interviewed. Those who were in a positive frame of mind for being interviewed and good speakers could easily respond to the interviewer's questions in a way that may described existing or non-existing systems in more tangible words. Those who felt harried, were physically tired may have been more curt and less thoughtful in their responses. Other managers who were interviewed may have had pressing work or personal concerns on their minds that distracted from the thoroughness and thoughtfulness of their responses. A fourth factor that may have influenced the research would be rating errors by the author. Marshall and Rossman (1989) note that sometimes the author does not ask the right questions due to a lack of expertise or understanding of the technical jargon of the participant. Finally, some managers may have misunderstood one or more of the questions being asked, or responded in a context that was different from that which was intended. Any and all of these factors could have influenced the quality of the response and subsequently, the scores assigned to each manager's application of Simon's four systems.

SUMMARY

In this chapter a summary and discussion of the research findings have been presented. Analysis of preliminary organizational data indicated that the company has a business strategy in place along with a system of beliefs, boundaries, diagnostic and interactive control systems. These findings were also consistent for the semiconductor manufacturing division. Interviews were conducted with four senior managers, seven middle managers and twenty-six first-line managers. These individuals responded to the same twenty-six questions following a structured, open-ended approach. The interviews suggest that senior managers had all four of Simon's systems in place and that these systems supported the company business strategy. Interviews with middle managers indicated that most had some of Simon's systems in place to help support the division business strategy. However, a major difference between the responses given by middle management and senior management was the level of clarity provided. Both senior and middle managers appear to have complete systems in place that encompassed both the work itself (quantity and quality of work), and how the work was to be accomplished with others. A trend that ran through the first-line manager interviews was that of a highly tactical focus. First-line managers as a group were particularly weak in the areas of belief systems and alignment of all systems.

   The Spearman Coefficient of Correlation indicates there was a strong relationship between a middle manager's annual achievement and focal ranking, and a moderate relationship between the annual achievement and focal ranking of first-line managers. This same relationship was only moderate for first-line managers. These outcomes provided some evidence to support a conclusion that individuals who have a higher ability to utilize Simon's four systems are also rated higher on annual achievement and focal ranking.

A summary and discussion of the findings, implications and suggestions for further research will be presented in Chapter 5.

Findings and Conclusions

The purpose of this research was to examine if and to what extent successful senior, middle and first-line managers used belief, boundary, diagnostic and interactive control systems or similar systems to achieve high productivity and innovation in their areas of responsibility.

To compete effectively in today's business world, organizations must continually adapt to a wide variety of unpredictable, rapid, and often erratic environmental conditions such as changes in the workforce, society, competition, technology and organizational structures. Organizations that are unable to adapt will find it difficult to compete effectively by turning business opportunities into valued services and/or products for their customers. Managers have a great deal of responsibility for ensuring that the organization is productive and effective. In order for organizations to compete more effectively in a dynamic workplace, they need to reexamine traditional assumptions that inform how managers learn and apply the skills and knowledge needed to excel in both tactical and strategic issues on the job. Research conducted by Simons indicates that senior managers in various Fortune 500 companies achieved profitable growth by controlling and balancing the tension between creative innovation and the need for predictable goal achievement using four levers, or systems of control. Simons' research and subsequent model offers professionals and managers a context from which to apply specific and general managerial skills and knowledge in order to enhance both organizational productivity and managerial success on-the-job.

While Simon's research indicates that excellent senior managers utilized belief, boundary, diagnostic and interactive control systems, it does not indicate the extent or amount of time these managers spent on tasks or activities related to these systems. Further, Simons does not indicate if or to what extent middle or first line managers utilize these systems. This research attempted to address this shortcoming by examining if, and to what extent successful senior, middle and first-line managers at a high technology manufacturer used these four or similar systems of control in order to achieve high productivity and innovation in their areas of responsibility.

REVIEW OF THE SUPPORTING LITERATURE

A review of the contributors to four major models of management including the Rational Goal Model, Internal Process Model, Human Relations Model, Behavioral Model, and Open Systems Model was conducted to illustrate the pattern of growth that led to Simons model. Each of the four basic management models was defined and the contributions of each theorist were identified.

Simons' research and model of belief, boundary, diagnostic and interactive control systems offers managers a context from which to apply specific and general managerial skills and knowledge in a more strategic or transformational manner to enhance both organizational productivity and managerial success on-the-job. However, while Simon's research indicated that excellent senior managers utilized belief, boundary, diagnostic and interactive control systems, he did not indicate the extent or amount of time these managers spent on tasks or activities related to these systems. Further, Simons did not indicate if or to what extent middle or first line managers utilized these systems.

REVIEW OF THE METHODS AND PROCEDURES

A qualitative research methodology was followed in order to obtain an in-depth understanding of the way successful senior, middle and first-line managers utilize Simon's four systems or similar systems to achieve their business strategy. Data were collected using three approaches including obtaining preliminary organizational data, structured, open-ended interviews and written documentation. Additional documentation, provided by the Director of Human Resources, consisted of the middle and first-line manager's performance appraisals and focal rankings for the previous calendar year.

SUMMARY OF IMPORTANT FINDINGS

A number of important findings resulted from this research. These findings are presented by first reviewing the business strategy of the company, manufacturing division and each level of management, second by responding to each research question and third by summarizing specific findings that cross all research questions.

Findings Related to Business Strategy

The preliminary analysis of organizational data indicated the company and manufacturing division had a business strategy in place. A review of presentations made by senior executives, annual reports, Internet data and company publications indicated that the company set aggressive business objectives for 1997. These included increasing revenues from $2 billion to $3 billion, achieving new levels of technology, and attracting major new customers (Sanders, 1997). It appeared that these goals were a bit optimistic as revenues for 1997 only reached $2.4 billion. While the desired levels of technology were achieved, the rate at which these technologies were implemented was far slower than expected.

Table 29: Summary of Organization/Division Systems

System	Examples
Belief System	Vision, mission & values statements
	Purpose statement
Boundary System	Policies & Procedures
	Codes of conduct
	5–year strategic planning systems
	Operational guidelines
Diagnostic System	Major business indices
	Attainment to goal reviews
	Incentives tied to goal achievement
	Quality standards
Interactive Control System	Company/Division publications
	Operations Reviews
	Meetings & Annual Reviews

The company's strategies recognized the major 'drivers' of the high technology business environment including the need to develop products that met customer needs in terms of cost, cycle time, performance and complexity (Reinertsen, 1997). Further, the strategies recognized the need to partner with others through strategic alliances and joint ventures in order to meet company goals (Sayles, 1993). Joint ventures and partnerships were concluded with the Saxony government in Germany, Fujitsu in Japan, and the development of a test and assembly facility in China.

Both the company and manufacturing division also had systems of beliefs, boundaries, diagnostic and interactive control systems. These systems appeared reflective of those identified by Simons and summarized in Table 29.

While the company and division appeared to have the business strategy and systems advocated by Simons, there was some evidence that these systems were probably not as aligned and supportive of each other and the business strategy as one moved from the senior to the first-line management level (Hanna, 1988). Simons observed that the purpose of aligning business strategy and the four systems of control is to provide the basic processes for, "providing goals; telling people what they will be rewarded for; telling them what not to do; telling them what you believe in; asking for their ideas; sharing knowledge" (1995, p.175) The company and division belief statements advocate for achievement of long-term goals by focusing on the development of leaders who set direction, get results, and create a supportive environment (JTE Brochure, 1997). Analysis of the interviews and performance appraisals suggested that 'getting results' was clearly the primary focus at the first-line level. This suggested that the organization and division have the right outcomes in mind, but do not have an integrated process for assuring alignment of strategy, belief, boundary, diagnostic and interactive control systems throughout the organization. Current research suggests that for companies to excel, they must not be focused entirely on results, also create work environments that support any higher order outcomes that are desired (Kaplan & Norton, 1996; Collins & Porras, 1994).

Findings Relating to Research Questions

1. What belief systems undergird senior, middle and first-line manager strategy in achieving their organizational goals?

While all senior managers appeared to have a system of beliefs established, the evidence of this system became increasingly scarce as one moved to front-line management where only eleven of twenty-six managers had strong evidence of a belief system. It was also interesting to note that even among managers at any level who exhibited strong or very strong evidence of a belief system, there was little consistency between the beliefs or values of one management group and another. There was not a 'common set' of beliefs or values. Most had developed their own values statements, some used Zenger Miller Basic Principles, Covey's Seven Habits, and so on. However, it was important to note that in the past year, the company had formally articulated and published its values, and the manufacturing division began a coordinated training and alignment process for all employees and management.

2. What boundary systems do senior, middle, and first-line managers invoke through their management strategy in order to remain focused on organizational goals?

All levels of management appeared to have good boundary systems in place. Organization policies and procedures, codes of conduct and operational procedures guide much of the direction of activity. Performance reviews, operations reviews and meetings also serve to focus activity. In addition to the company boundaries, the division and each plant complies with ISO 9000 certification requirements. This extensive process requires that certified organizations undergo an auditing process on a yearly basis to ensure that the company is living up to the quality standards it promotes. The result is a continuous improvement effort that was documented by detailed policies, specifications and procedures. There was general agreement across all management levels that boundaries were well monitored and that appropriate time was spent monitoring boundaries.

3. What diagnostic control systems do senior, middle, and first-line managers use to monitor and predict quality and productivity?

The diagnostic systems were the most prevalent across all management groups. This was probably in part due to the nature of the manufacturing environment and the automated systems that are in place which measure every step and stage in the manufacturing process. A common response to questions on this system included a first-line manager who said, "Measurement is our bread and butter. We are engineers, so that is what comes naturally to us. We measure everything." The validity of this manager's response was readily evident by the stacks of diagnostic reports that were stacked in most manager's offices. Because of the sheer volume of information available, the danger in this area for a manager was to ensure they are focusing on the right data, and not becoming overwhelmed with too much data.

4. What interactive control systems do senior, middle, and first-line managers employ to ensure predictable goal achievement?

As with belief systems, the interactive control systems were strongest in senior and middle management levels, and weakest in the first-line management level. Senior and middle managers appeared to have the best understanding of the need to meet with direct reports to both stay informed and convey what was important. Senior and middle managers generally met daily with their direct reports and frequently with problem solving or continuous improvement work groups. While all twenty-six first-line managers reported involving themselves in the decisions and planning activities of their subordinates through staff meetings, 1:1 meetings, performance reviews and passdowns, their ability to articulate the purpose of these activities was weak. For example, ten first-line managers simply noted that they 'attended meetings' but could not articulate how they influenced decision-making of subordinates.

5. How do senior, middle, and first-line managers use belief systems, boundary systems, interactive control systems, and diagnostic control systems to link to the business strategy of the company?

Senior and middle management specified that they considered three components to ensure alignment between their systems and the company business strategy. These three components were setting direction, setting and tracking attainment to goals, and communicating this information to subordinates and superiors. Of the twenty-six first-line managers, only six could articulate how they integrated their business strategy and systems. The responses provided by this management level suggest that their focus was largely tactical and short-term. It also suggests that while the organization espouses a desire to ensure goal and activity alignment throughout the organization, first-line managers are not clear about how to accomplish this alignment. Rather, they may not be very familiar with the higher level business strategy and how to ensure alignment from their level in the organization on up to the module or division level. If this is correct, it first suggests that neither senior nor middle managers are effective at ensuring this level of understanding among first-line managers. Second, it would suggest that middle managers are not actively coaching or mentoring their first-line direct reports regarding the module, division and company strategic business plans. As a result, the focus at the first-line level becomes quite tactical. One could assume that if a large portion of the first-line management do not understand and cannot articulate how their strategy supports that of the larger organization, their direct reports are equally confused.

Other Important Findings

There were a number of general findings that cross all of the research questions.

- Interview and documentation data indicate that senior managers tend to have a business strategy that is supported by Simons' four systems. However, the communication of this strategy to the first-line manager level could be improved.
- There was a moderate relationship between middle manager systems average and annual review (0.55), and focal ranking (0.66). There was also a moderate relationship between first-line manager systems average and annual review (0.45) and focal ranking (0.59). These data were determined by computing a Spearman Rho correlation of coefficient to determine to what extent the variables were related.
- There was a strong relationship between a middle manager's annual achievement and focal ranking (0.89), and a moderate relationship between the annual achievement and focal ranking

(0.66) of first-line managers. These data were also determined by computing a Spearman Rho correlation of coefficient to determine to what extent the variables were related.

These outcomes provided some evidence to support a conclusion that managers at any level who had the ability to establish an appropriate business strategy and utilize Simon's four systems were more likely to be rated higher on annual achievement and focal ranking.

- There were no additional systems identified in this research that would add to the four identified by Simons. The research did indicate that the organization and division's ability to implement its strategies and beliefs from the senior to the first-line level can be strengthened.
- At the senior and middle management levels, the ability to set direction, get results and develop a supportive environment were valued. At the first line level, these same qualities were rarely mentioned. Instead, first-line managers placed a high value on one's technical skill and the ability to get results was the most highly valued competency.

INTERPRETATIONS

These data indicated that individuals who had the ability to conceptualize and apply Simons' four systems and align those systems with the company business strategy were more likely to be rated higher on both performance appraisal and focal ranking. Correlation's suggested that there was a moderate relationship (Rho = 0.55) between annual review and systems average, and focal ranking and systems average (Rho = 0.66) among middle managers. Correlation's also suggested a moderate relationship (Rho = 0.45) between annual review and systems average, and focal ranking and systems average (Rho = 0.59) among first-line managers.

A second implication of this research was that the higher in the organization one's position, the greater the likelihood that one was familiar with, and had developed a business strategy that supported and was aligned with the business strategy of the larger organization. It also appeared that the higher in the organization one's position, the greater the likelihood that one would have one or more of the four control systems in place. The results suggested that senior management had the greatest familiarity and alignment with the company business strategy while the familiarity and alignment with the company business strategy for middle managers was moderately strong. The results also suggested that at the first-line level, a short-term, results-oriented perspective was the norm. Hence, their level of familiarity and alignment with the business strategy of the larger organization was less evident. The fact that the level of business strategy, systems and alignment decrease as one moved from senior to first-line management may be a function of the expected roles and responsibilities at each level. Traditionally, first-line managers in a manufacturing setting are tasked with maintaining production of the manufacturing line. Due to the nature of the manufacturing process, it may be that a short-term focus may be appropriate for most work. It may also be that the first-line manager 'business strategy' really is determined at the senior and middle management level, for implementation at the middle and first-line management level. If this is true, then a 'nose-to-the-grindstone' perspective may be appropriate. On the other hand, it could also be true that all or most first-line managers just do not know how to develop a business strategy or systems aligned to that of the larger organization that is appropriate for their management level. A contributing factor may be that senior and middle management are not acting as mentors and models to help develop these skills in first-line management. Finally, it may also be that the organizational systems do not recognize or reward first-line managers to spend the time and effort necessary to develop a business strategy and supportive systems.

Company and division documentation and some activities (training, peer reviews, senior management presentations, etc.) strongly suggested that managers that lead by setting direction, getting results and creating a supportive environment are desired. However, these same data also suggested that 'getting results' was primarily what was explicitly and overtly rewarded. Both the senior and middle management ranks stressed the importance of getting results in addition to working well with others. The first-line managers, on the other hand, stressed technical competence and 'meeting the numbers' as their primary area of focus. Setting direction and creating a supportive environment were not major considerations for first-line managers. It would seem that the message of what upper management says it desired, and what it was actually getting at the first-line level was not consistent. If this was in fact what was happening, it is likely that workers who report to first-line managers were also not clear about how their work was aligned with and supportive of the business strategy of the larger organization.

SUPPORTING LITERATURE

The author's interpretation of these findings are supported by many articles in the literature. The first interpretation above suggests that individuals who applied Simons' four systems and aligned those systems with the company's business strategy were more likely to be rated higher on both performance appraisal and focal ranking. This finding may be explained from several possible vantage points. Some scholars (Wells, 1997, Barach & Eckhardt, 1996; Senge, 1990) argue that managers can learn to improve their capacity to deal with multiple systems. Murphy (1997) suggests eight major roles managers as leaders fulfill which can fall within the systems identified by Simons. Morecroft and Sterman (1994) agree noting that managers can learn to investigate, conceptualize and transfer learning regarding more complex systems through the creation of artificial 'microworlds' or simulations.

Some research would indicate that one's ability to learn and apply more complex systems may be limited. For example, Herbert Simon's theory of bounded rationality suggests that a manager may be inherently limited in "both knowledge and computational capacity" (1997, p. 291). Jaques (1989) also argues that the nature of work and one's ability to deal with increasing complexity in terms of time, work and span of control varies considerably among individuals.

A solution that would encompass both view points might be to offer the opportunity for managers to increase their capacity and ability to become familiar with and align with the company's business strategy and to develop balanced, integrated systems of control for their level of management. If as Jaques and Simons argue, capacity is limited, those who are better able to effectively multi-task and develop balanced, integrated systems with their business strategy will rise to the top. On the other hand, there is also evidence that managerial training and organizational systems simply do not provide the opportunities for managers to develop this increased capacity and ability. "Our bottom line is that good executives don't grow on trees. They are 'grown' by responsible corporations that provide, over a period of many years, the nurturing and developmental experiences necessary to equip the individuals to master the ultimate executive responsibilities" (Potts & Sykes, 1993, p. 12). If this is the case, improved processes for assisting managers to develop should be implemented.

A second implication of this research was that the higher in the organization one's position, the greater the likelihood that one had become familiar with the business strategy, and one or more of the four control systems in place. It is important to note that Simons also observed that a given business strategy and systems is no guarantee of success. Barach and Eckhardt (1996) observe that the responsibilities of senior managers include establishing the structure of the organization and the systems that encourage, motivate and control behavior. They go on to note that middle managers must begin to develop these same skill sets and learn to apply them in the workplace if they are to advance. Potts and Sykes (1996) also observe that those individuals who are better able to provide a good work environment that is integrated with and supportive of the business strategy, build team effectiveness, motivate through vision, mission and purpose, and implement systems that support these efforts tend to advance within organizations.

The final implication discussed suggests that what upper management said it desired and what it was getting at the first-line level was not consistent. Zaleznik (1997, p. 54) notes that "Managers are measured by how well they get people to go along with the company's expectations, not by how well the company performs." In this case, it appeared that lower levels of management believed that they are measured, and ultimately rewarded, for short-term results. Argyris identifies this dynamic as a situation in which "Organizational defensive routines encourage individuals to bypass the causes of [an incompatible or misaligned system] and to cover up the bypass. They also encourage making this action undiscussable and the undiscussability undiscussable" (1997, p. 368). The detrimental effect of saying one thing and doing another is noted in the following statement. "If the leader has conflicts, such as wanting a team-based consensus process for decision making and, at the same time, wanting to maintain complete control and reward subordinates for individual prowess in solving problems, we will see inconsistent policies regarding decision making, incentives and rewards" (Schein, 1997, p.

61.). Schein goes on to observe that once these inconsistencies become embedded in the organization's culture, they are difficult to overcome.

DISCUSSION OF PROBLEMS & LIMITATIONS

There were a number of problems and limitations that were encountered in the process of implementing this research study which should be considered when interpreting these results and should be dealt with when continuing this type of research. Obvious concerns included any threats to validity and reliability. Several steps were taken to ensure the validity and reliability of the research analysis. First, validity and reliability can be obtained in qualitative research by validating the data against the literature (Strauss & Corbin, 1990). As the previous section describing the supporting literature indicates, there is a sizable body of research that supports the findings of this research. A second method for ensuring validity and reliability included having the respondents verify the accuracy of the findings (Yin, 1994; Strauss & Corbin, 1990). To verify the accuracy of the findings, the author presented the findings to three groups of manufacturing division managers. These included the division Learning and Development Council, composed of senior and middle-level managers, the Middle manager Council, composed of middle management, and the First-line manager Forum, is composed of first-line managers. The same presentation was given to each group and included an overview of the purpose of the research, the research questions, a brief literature review, a description of the methodology and the findings. Feedback from these groups was fairly consistent in that the findings were validated. Comments included, "Well, I guess in hindsight this shouldn't be too much of a surprise," and "I wouldn't have thought it was so wide, but the alignment of our strategy from top to bottom sure does need some work." Feedback and suggestions from these councils are being compiled and used to improve the quality of training and on-the-job learning opportunities within the manufacturing division. Efforts were also taken to corroborate the findings and observations to raw data by triangulating the data to documents, interviews and observations (Patton, 1990). The results of corroboration was evident in the descriptions of company and division documentation, tables of interview results and participant quotations.

A third limitation related to the small sample size. Given the small sample size, it is not possible to generalize the results to a larger population. As this sample does not reflect the general demographic mix of the American workforce or the company, no generalizations are being drawn that are ascribed to any setting other than the manufacturing division. A solution to this problem would be to include a larger sample across all manager levels from several organizations; perhaps conducting survey or multiple case study results.

A fourth limitation was that the qualitative case study approach relying on open-ended question can be viewed as a lack of rigor compared to traditional descriptive research methods. Although each individual was asked the same questions, there was no way of knowing if the issue embedded in that question was of importance to the individual, unimportant, or that they simply misunderstood the question. In any case, the data was accurately recorded and even though the sample was small, the data represent a variety of views and may increase understanding. In addition, the frequencies of responses to the questions have been fairly reported and thus the ability to generalize may be judged by the reader from the size of the sample and the clarity of the description. Guba and Lincoln note that these limitations are overcome by careful, documented data gathering, coding and analytical procedures (1985).

A fifth problem that was encountered concerned the business environment that the organization and manufacturing division were in during the time of this research. When the research began, the organization was expecting a highly profitable year with revenues increasing from $2 billion to $3 billion in sales. In reality, due to problems with achieving the level of technology needed to ensure high quality and high volume productivity, the organization expects to achieve sales of only $2.5 billion. The net effect of these problems required the manufacturing division to undergo a substantial change. A large proportion of the senior, middle and first-line management moved to new units and/or lost large numbers of staff in transfers. While the participants at the senior, middle and first-line levels had been at their current job status for at least one year, many had only recently moved to a new unit, and were under very strong pressure to focus on manufacturing indices. This environment may have affected the quality of the answers provided during the interviews. Additional research could focus on selecting an organization that is in a stable business cycle.

PRACTICAL IMPLICATIONS

Managers play a critical role in an organization's ability to meet its strategic business objectives, maintain daily operations and facilitate positive change and learning within the workforce. This research pointed to a number of practical approaches learning professionals, organization development professionals and management might take to enhance the development of managers.

Training that does not achieve the intended results is a waste of valuable time, funding and resources. Research has shown that much of the time spent in training is not transferred to the workplace. Robinson and Robinson (1989) demonstrated that managers who did not see a payoff for using new skills, not having confidence in the new skills, or not seeing an application were less inclined to use those skills on-the-job. The traditional methods of teaching management skills (one topic at a time) through lecture, guided discussions, and role-plays may not be as effective as is needed in today's dynamic business environment. New methods that require clear understanding of the purpose, development and integration of one's business strategy, belief, boundary, diagnostic and interactive systems is needed. Further, managers need to be prompted to consider how to balance and integrate these systems with the business strategy. Mentoring, coaching of on-the-job development, and structured 'real-world' experiences or simulations may offer ways of developing managers abilities to achieve this high level of understanding and application. For this level of learning to be worthwhile, it must be accomplished within the constant bustle of day-to-day events in the workplace.

Training and organization development professionals should help to evaluate, modify and/or establish organizational systems and processes that help to ensure the alignment of the larger business strategy down to the first-line management level. These systems and processes should ensure that managers who are best able to develop appropriate control systems that are aligned and supportive of the business strategy are rewarded and recognized.

Finally, managers at all levels should take a more critically reflective role in their own development. Where in the past they may have been content to passively attend various 'how-to-manage' classes, they must now begin to insist that *their* managers take time to provide coaching and mentoring on a routine basis. Coaching and mentoring could be focused on a wide range of topics and skills depending on the individual manager's needs. Managers also need to be more vocal in identifying when systems are not in alignment with stated objectives, and more aggressive in collaborating with support staff to design systems that do reward, recognize and support managerial and leadership development.

SUGGESTIONS FOR FURTHER RESEARCH

As a result of this study, several possible areas of future research became evident. While in no way conclusive, the results of this work add to the growing body of knowledge indicating that the systems and processes of organizations strongly influence the way in which managers manage, and ultimately, the success of the organization. One suggestion for further research would be to include a larger sample across all management grades from several high technology manufacturing organizations. An alternative could be to study larger groups at a single management level. Either approach would provide additional data from which generalizations could be made.

The effect of experience over time is also a factor that could affect the development of individuals in management positions. Future researchers may want to consider time and experience from two perspectives. First, it may be interesting to consider how much actual management experience an individual has accumulated. This research study required participants to have been in their position for at least one year. Some may have been managing for one year, some for a number of years providing these latter individuals with time to learn to develop a business strategy, systems and align those systems. Second, future researchers may want to explore how senior, middle and first-line managers develop their ability to become familiar with and align to a company's business strategy over time. Where this research looked at a sample of participants as a single snap-shot in time, future research may follow a group of managers over a longer time frame to determine if and how some become more familiar with the company's business strategy, and then develop systems aligned with that strategy. Third, future research may want to consider how the provision or non-existence of structured, targeted mentoring and coaching from one's immediate manager may help improve development. A final suggestion for future research would be to study how systems within the organization support, remain aligned or break down from the level of the larger organization, to senior, middle and first-line management. This research suggests that there is a breakdown in the larger organization's desire to develop leaders focused on the long-term, and the actual practice of first-line managers who are primarily focused on getting results over the short-term. There may be some dynamics that can be remedied to address this discrepancy.

SUMMARY

The purpose of this research has been to examine if and to what extent successful senior, middle and first-line managers use belief, boundary, diagnostic and interactive control systems or similar systems to achieve high productivity and innovation in their areas of responsibility. This chapter has presented a summary and discussion of the findings, implications and suggestions for further research. Charles Handy observed that, "Change does not have to be forced on us by crisis and calamity. We can do it for ourselves," and "Those who are always learning are those who can ride the waves of change and see a changing world as full of opportunities rather than of damages" (1989, p. 56). This effort has resulted in change and learning from two vantage points. First, it has contributed to the body of knowledge relating to managerial learning and organizational change. This has been discussed in depth in the previous paragraphs. Second, it was noted earlier that qualitative research method assumes an interaction between the author and those participating in the research. Accordingly, it is important to note that this effort allowed the author the opportunity to meet with and learn from the views, philosophies, strategies and tactics of a varied and talented group of managers. From each, the author was able to learn new techniques, perspectives and insights to apply to his own management style. From each, this author was able to identify gaps in his own unit strategy, belief, boundary, diagnostic and interactive control systems. Collectively, discovering what worked and did not work for these managers also aided the author as an internal change agent influencing both learning and organizational adaptation. Managers in this and other organizations have high standards and expectations to live up to in order to assist organizations in the dynamic, exciting times we face currently and in the future. The time for change is upon us. The time for learning is now.

Interview Questions

INTRODUCTION

Thank you for taking this time to meet with me. As you know, [the company] and division are interested in developing the leadership abilities of individuals within management. The results of this interview will be used to help identify how senior, middle and first-line manager set direction, get results and create a supportive environment within the areas of their responsibility.

You were selected by random sample as one of approximately 38 participants in this effort. The questions I will be asking regard your role as a manager and how that role supports the business strategy of your (division, plant, module, shift). I may be asking for some documentation regarding your business strategy or activities as we go along.

I will be recording this interview to ensure that your comments are accurately reflected. If you do not feel comfortable with your interview being recorded, I will summarize your comments in written form. All information that is obtained in connection with this study that can be identified with you will remain confidential and disclosed only with your permission. The results of the interviews and any documentation will be collated to maintain the anonymity for all participants. Copies of the audio-tapes, individual interviews and documentation will be kept in a secured file by [the author] and destroyed after the results are compiled.

If you prefer not to participate please let me know. Even if you decide to participate, you are free to discontinue your participation at any time.

If you have questions or think of additional issues later, please call [the author] at [phone number]. Any questions before we start?

OPENING QUESTIONS

1. Think about your highest performing direct report. What criteria do you use to rate that person so highly?
2. What criteria indicates that an individual is ready for promotion to your level?
3. Think about a direct report who has been in his/her job for at least one year & needs the *most improvement*. What criteria do you use to rate that individual as needing the *most improvement*?
4. What criteria do you feel indicates that a direct report is not qualified for the position he/she holds?

BUSINESS STRATEGY

5. What is the business strategy for your (division, plant, module, shift)?

BELIEF SYSTEM

6. Do your direct reports have organizational values, purpose & direction that guide their job performance and interactions with others and support your business strategy? (Evidence)
7. What major job tasks must you accomplish to personally convey the organizational values, purpose & direction to the individuals who work for you in order to support your business strategy?
8. What percent of your time in a week do you feel you personally spend conveying organizational values, purpose and direction to your reports in order to support your business strategy? Why?
9. Do you feel you are allocating the right amount of time to covey your organizational values, purpose & direction in order to support your business strategy?
10. What percent of time should management above you be allocating to this conveying organizational values, purpose & direction in order to support their business strategy? Why?

BOUNDARY SYSTEMS

11. How do your reports know what to focus their job activities on in order to achieve the business strategy? (Evidence)
12. What major job tasks must you accomplish to ensure that your direct reports are focused on the right activities needed to achieve your business strategy?
13. What percent of your time in a week do you personally spend ensuring your direct reports are focused on the right activities needed to achieve your business strategy? Why?
14. Do you feel you are spending the right amount of time ensuring your reports are focused on the right activities needed to achieve your business strategy? Why or Why not?
15. What percent of their time should management above and below you personally spend ensuring that their direct reports are focused on the right activities needed to achieve your business strategy?

DIAGNOSTIC SYSTEMS

16. How do you monitor organizational metrics related to your business strategy & correcting any deviations from preset standards of performance? (Evidence)
17. What major job tasks must you accomplish to monitor organizational metrics & correct deviations in order to achieve your business strategy?
18. What percent of your time in a week do you feel you personally allocate to monitoring outcomes and correcting deviations in order to achieve your business strategy?
19. Do you feel you are allocating the right amount of time monitoring outcomes & correcting deviations to achieve your business strategy this system? Why or Why not?
20. What percent of their time should management above & below you be personally spending to monitor organizational outcomes & correct for deviations?

INTERACTIVE CONTROL SYSTEMS

21. How do you involve yourself in the decisions and planning activities of your direct reports in order to achieve your business strategy?

22. What major job tasks must you accomplish to involve yourself in the decisions & planning activities of your direct reports in order to achieve your business strategy?

23. What percent of your time in a week do you feel you personally allocate to involve yourself in the decisions and planning activities of your direct reports in order to achieve your business strategy? Why?

24. Do you feel you are allocating the right amount of time to involving yourself in the decisions and planning activities of your direct reports in order to achieve your business strategy? Why or Why not?

25. What percent of their time do you think management above and below you should be allocating to involve themselves in the decisions and planning activities of their direct reports in order to achieve their business strategy? Why?

CONCLUDING

26. We have discussed how your use values, boundaries, metrics and involvement to support your business strategy. How do you ensure that these four elements also support or align with each other?

27. Are there any other points you would like to make that would help me understand how you achieve your business plan?

CONCLUSION

Thanks for taking this time- I appreciate your willingness to share your insights into your role as a manager and how to achieve your business strategy. Let me remind you that if you have questions or think of additional issues that pertain to this interview later, please call me at [phone number].

Research Cover Letter

INTEROFFICE MEMO

To: Manufacturing Division Leadership Participant
From: The Author
Date: Month, Day, 1997
Re: Division Leadership Research

You are invited to participate in a study of how managers align their beliefs, boundary, diagnostic and interactive communication systems with business strategy. I hope to learn how senior, middle and first-line managers integrate management systems in support of business strategy. You were selected by random sample as one of approximately 38 participants in this study because of your status as a manager at [the company].

If you decide to participate, I will be meeting with you for approximately 90 minutes to conduct an interview regarding the nature of your role as a manager and how that role supports business strategy. The interview will not require any special preparation on your part and you do not have to answer every question. You may be asked to provide some documentation regarding business strategy, communication plans or project plans during the course of the interview. If it is not convenient to provide documentation at that time, I can follow up with you at a time that is convenient. The interview will be recorded to ensure that your comments are accurately reflected. If you aren't comfortable with your interview being recorded, I will conduct the interview and summarize your responses in written notes. As a result of the interview, you may find that you have a better idea of how your role as a manager supports business strategy. If it is not practical to have an interview conducted with you in person, I will be glad to conduct the interview by telephone.

Any information that is obtained in connection with this study and that can be identified with you will remain confidential and will be disclosed only with your permission. The results of the interviews will be collated such that anonymity for all participants will be maintained. The names of participants will not be used in reporting the data. Copies of audio-tapes and notes will be kept in a secure file by the researcher and destroyed upon graduation.

Your decision whether or not to participate will not affect your future relations with [the company]. If you decide to participate, you are free to discontinue participation at any time.

If you have any additional questions later, please call me and I will be glad to answer them. You may keep a copy of this form if you desire.

Annual Achievement Summary

ANNUAL ACHIEVEMENT SUMMARY

Employee Name	_____	Dept. No: _____	Evaluation Period: _____ to _____

Employee Badge # _____

Job Code _____   Job Title: _____   Supervisor/Manager: _____

GOAL ACHIEVEMENT SUMMARY:
Supervisor/Manager comments on overall performance against goals for the year, highlighting major accomplishments and areas in which further development would benefit both the employee and the success of the organization. (Attach additional sheet if necessary)

MAJOR ACCOMPLISHMENTS:

DEVELOPMENT AREAS:

Quarterly Frequency
Goals & Achievement Score: (Attach completed G&A forms). *Total Goal Achievement <u>must</u> be annualized.

	Q1	Q2	Q3	Q4	*Total Goal Achievement
4=Exceptional Contribution					
3=Successful Contribution					
2=Some Contribution					
1=Inadequate Contribution	4 pts. max.	4 pts. max.	4 pts. max.	4 pts. max.	16 pts. max. (Copy to Back)

Semi-Annual Frequency
Goals & Achievement Scores: (Attach completed G&A forms). *Total Goal Achievement <u>must</u> be annualized.

	Q1/Q2		Q3/Q4		*Total Goal Achievement
4=Exceptional Contribution		+		X 2	
3=Successful Contribution					
2=Some Contribution					
1=Inadequate Contribution	4 pts. max.		4 pts. max.		16 pts. max. (Copy to Back)

CORPORATE AND DIVISION SUCCESS FACTORS: Company values (Respect for people, Integrity & Responsibility, Competition, Knowledge, Initiative & Accountability, and Our Customers' Success) are embedded in the following success factors. Supervisor/Manager comments on employee performance in the areas listed below:

1. CONTINUOUS IMPROVEMENT: Offering & supporting ideas to increase productivity. *Key Skills: strategic thinking, initiative, flexibility, leadership.*

2. TEAMWORK: Competing as a team to improve products & both individual & group performance. *Key Skills: cooperation, active participation, mutual respect and recognition.*

3. COMMUNICATION: Respecting individual differences & seeking understanding. *Key Skills: listening, sharing knowledge/information, providing feedback, and influencing others.*

4. PROBLEM SOLVING: Taking initiative to recognize obstacles and create solutions. *Key skills: data analysis, planning, organizing and taking responsibility for results.*

5. CUSTOMER SUCCESS: Making it easy for customers to do business with us. Taking action to further customer success. *Key skills: listening, responsiveness, follow-through, being proactive, offering suggestions and insight. (Use actual customer feedback when writing this portion of the review.)*

6. JOB/COMPANY KNOWLEDGE: Ongoing learning in order to enhance company and personal growth. *Key skills: understanding of company's core businesses, customers, and competitors; increasing professional and technical knowledge, applying learning in the workplace, sharing knowledge with co-workers; appreciating change.*

7. OTHER(S) (specific to the division, dept. or job):

Success Factor Achievement: (Circle one. Transfer below.)

7 – 8 = Exceptional:	Leader. Significant contributor to achievement of company's evolving business needs. Models company values.
5 – 6 = Successful:	Consistent contributor. Acts to meet company's current business needs and strives to live the company values.
3 – 4 = Developing:	Showing improvement. Needs development on success factors to realize potential and meet company's business needs. Understands the company values.
1 – 2 = Inadequate:	Negative impact. May be counter-productive to company's business needs or inconsistent with company values.

ANNUAL ACHIEVEMENT TOTAL:

TOTAL GOAL ACHIEVEMENT: ___ /16 pts.
SUCCESS FACTOR ACHIEVEMENT: ___ /8 pts.
ANNUAL TOTAL: ___ /24 pts.

OVERALL RATING: (Check One)

21-24 pts.:	EXCEPTIONAL ACHIEVEMENT
16-20 pts.:	SUCCESSFUL ACHIEVEMENT
11-15 pts.:	IMPROVEMENT REQUIRED
5-10 pts.:	DOES NOT MEET EXPECTATIONS

EMPLOYEE COMMENTS:

(attach additional sheet)

Manager Signature ___ Date ___

*Employee Signature ___ Date ___

*This evaluation has been completed as a tool to help you in your job performance and development. Your signature does not necessarily indicate agreement with the rating, but simply that your supervisor or manager has discussed it with you.

Next Level Manager ___ Date ___

SEND THIS FORM (WITH GOALS & ACHIEVEMENT FORMS ATTACHED) TO RECORDS UPON COMPLETION

APPENDIX D
Company Data

Results of Preliminary Data Analysis - Company

Business Strategy	Beliefs	Boundaries	Diagnostics	Interactive Controls
1997 Objectives	Fairness-Opportunity-	Integrated circuits	$ growth,	Tools for communication:
$3 billion in revenues	Need to grow expertise in software	Programmable products in concert with applications solutions	Profit and Loss	Dialog
Achieve operating profitability in Q1	Community involvement (be a good community citizen)	Provide to manufacturers of equipment for personal and networked computation and communication	Sales	Breakfasts
Achieve positive EVA by Q4 for each of the major product areas	People are the ultimate source of our competitive advantage	Human Resource Policies and Procedures	Strategic plans	Employee update video's
Increase flash operating profit by 50% over 1996	Purpose Statement	Company Worldwide Standards of Business Conduct	Market share	Advances
$1 billion in microprocessor sales	Vision Statement		Plant capacity	Company TV
Vantis as a wholly-owned subsidiary	Mission Statement		Products produced	News letters
Sample customers with cell-based design Gigabit Ethernet Repeater Product	Values:		Patents awarded	Viewpoints
Ship products from Plant 25 utilizing CS44E	Respect for people		Budgets	External:
Announce notebook using microprocessor with at least two top-tier manufacturers	Integrity and responsibility		Transistor density (10-15 million per chip)	Sematech
Strategies:	Competition		Building systems or subsystems on a chip	Conferences
Customer service	Knowledge		Grow faster & earn higher rate of return than semiconductor industry as a whole	Semiconductor Industry Asso.
Shorten time to market	Initiative and accountability			Joint ventures
Reduce costs	Our customers' success			Subscriptions to journals
Strategic alliances/joint ventures				Technical library
Solutions provider				Internal education
Supply critical technology				External education
30% market share in Windows compatible microprocessors by 1999				Conferences/Workgroups
				VP Conference
				Director's Conference
				Company Culture Team
				Company Leadership Team
				Recognition
				President's Spotlight
				VP Spotlight
				Recognition trips
				Sabbaticals
				Stock awards & Bonuses

Company Purpose, Vision, Mission & Values

Purpose: We empower people everywhere to lead more productive lives.

Vision: We at [the company] share a vision of a world that is enhanced through information technology, which liberates the human mind and spirit. [The company] is a leading supplier of critical enabling technology for the Information Age. In concert with our customers, we empower people everywhere to lead more productive lives by creating, processing & communicating information & knowledge. We are our customers' favorite integrated circuit supplier. With a strong commitment to our core values & mission, we anticipate & respond quickly to changing customer needs while preserving a culture that brings out the best in each of us.

Mission: [The company] produces integrated circuits, providing programmable products in concert with applications solutions to manufacturers of equipment for personal and networked computation and communication. To achieve success, [the company] combines innovative concepts with leadership in process technology and design and manufacturing excellence to offer products and services that reduce the cost, improve the performance and shorten the time to market for out target customers worldwide.

Values: We at [the company] are the guardians of the values that underlie our culture. The culture of [the company] is characterized by an indomitable will to persevere and prosper in one of the world's most competitive industries. The central tenant of our culture is a belief that people are the ultimate source of our competitive advantage. [Company] employees work hard, have fun, and celebrate our successes. Respect for people- honoring their rights as individuals- is the cornerstone of our culture. We respect individual differences and diversity as qualities that enhance our efforts as a team. We believe in treating each other fairly. Fairness is based on *what* is right, not *who* is right.

Integrity and Responsibility: We are committed to the highest standards of integrity in all aspects of our business and are responsible to all of our stakeholders. Our actions, as individuals and as a corporate citizen, enhance the quality of life and protect the environment of the communities in which we do business.

Competition: We believe that competition is the ultimate driving force of growth & progress. We compete as a team. We are driven by our competitive nature to achieve continuous improvement in our products, our individual performance, and in the contributions of our work teams.

Knowledge: We value learning as a lifelong process, the means by which we gain the knowledge to understand change, champion better ideas, improve productivity, & achieve both personal & corporate growth.

Initiative and Accountability: We take the initiative to identify obstacles to success & create solutions. We hold ourselves accountable for meeting our commitments. We take calculated risks to achieve our goals. We pursue excellence, as individuals & as a corporation, in everything we do.

Our Customers' Success: Our customers' success is our success. We offer innovative products and services that enhance the competitiveness of our customers. We seek to create and maintain lasting relationships based on trust and shared vision. We are committed to making it easy for our customers to do business with [the company].

Division Data

Results of Preliminary Data Analysis - Manufacturing Division

Business Strategy	Beliefs	Boundaries	Diagnostics	Interactive Controls
Division Goals	JTE principles	Align of division, plant, module & shift goals	High volume	Tools for communication:
Maintain manufacturing capacity to support customer demands	Insure customers drive quality	Process, equipment & facility under statistical control	High technology	JTE Newsletter
Achieve quarterly operating plans in all plants	Treat everything as a process	Ultraclean, ultrapure standards	Cost competitive	Dialog
Qualify & develop new technologies on schedule	Improve continuously	Automated distribution	Zero reliability failure	Company TV
Provide direction to achieve Leadership and Performance	Build in quality from the start	Virtually no inactive work-in-process	High yields (FY=97%, SY = 90%)	Update video's
Management Thrust goals	Solve problems using facts and data	No re-works	Defect density < 1/ sq inch	External:
Develop plant 25 to capacity to achieve $1 billion revenue	Involve everyone	Interconnected machine sets	Yield ramp to full maturity in 6 mo's	SEMATECH
Strategies:	Lead through active management	Paperless	Cycle time at 1.5x theoretical	Semiconductor Asso.
Exceed customer expectations (internal and external)	People & learning are critical to our success	Zero emissions	Equipment utilization of 80%	Conferences
Continuous learning	Social & technical systems must be optimized together	Safety	100% output to mix	Journals/periodicals
Continuous improvement	People are resources to be developed			External education
Cutting edge Human Resource practices	Organization is flat			Conferences/Workgroups
Team development	Employees are empowered			Core Steering Committee
Empower individuals	New ideas are encouraged			Learning Council
Supervisors & managers serve as coaches	Employees are cross-trained, multiskilled and flexible			Middle Manager Forum
Modular org. design	Information goes directly to the point of action			1st Line Manager Forum
Key facilitation of learning by division personnel				Thrust teams
				Peer Review Improvement Team
				Communications
				Re-alignment sessions
				Recognition Dinner
				Spotlights
				Merchandise
				Focus groups
				Employee breakfasts
				Pay & promotion

Cumulative Systems, Performance Appraisal and Focal Rankings

Middle Manager: Cumulative Systems, Performance Appraisal & Focal Rankings

Middle Manager	Bus. Strat	Belief	Bound	Diag	Inter Act.	Align-ment	Avg.	Performance Appraisal Language	Ann. Achiev	Focal Ranking
V2	4	4	5	6	5	4	4.7	Technically competent; analytical, data-driven, understands engineering design, assumed leadership role, thinks strategically, long-term fixes, team leader develops others, responsive to customers	22	3
W2	4	3	4	5	4	4	4.0	Tracks production metrics, continuous improvement, implemented checklists, team contributor, systematic at solving problems, excellent follow-through	21	5
Z2	4	3	5	6	5	5	4.7	Made upgrades, led team, met or exceeded goals, resolved technology issues, initiative, flexibility, organized, proactive, responsive	21	2
A3	6	4	6	6	6	6	5.7	Technically skilled, implemented many improvements, significantly reduced defects, dropped rework, communicates well, teamwork is exemplary, develops others	21	4
B3	5	3	6	6	5	5	5.0	Substantial improvements, enhanced systems, conceived, planned & implemented cultural change, led numerous initiatives, highly respected, proactive problem solver, major force, outstanding follow-through	22.6	1
C3	4	3	5	6	5	4	4.5	Implemented goals with good results, major contributor, led team, excellent job of cost control, supports JTE teams, follows-through, technical leader, fixes problems with data	19.9	7
D3	5	2	5	6	5	4	4.5	Expenses understood & controlled, well-functioning team, misprocessing greatly reduced, supports new technologies, excellent job improvement, good communicator, excellent team player, very job knowledgeable	20.2	6

First-Line Manager: Cumulative Systems, Performance Appraisal & Focal Rankings

1st-Line Manager	Bus. Strat	Belief	Bound	Diag	Inter Act.	Align-ment	Avg.	Performance Appraisal Language	Ann. Achiev.	Focal Ranking
A1	5	4	5	5	5	4	4.7	Effective manager, supports 'big picture,' leader of outstanding effort, technically skilled, strong team leader, excellent communicator	20.2	16
B1	3	5	5	6	4	4	4.5	Met goals, developing team, made significant improvements, problem-solving has improved, valuable member of team	20.0	8
E1	5	3	5	5	4	4	4.3	Increased knowledge, supported improvements, trained staff, has effective team, good problem-solver, proactive	19.9	19
H1	5	4	5	5	4	4	4.5	Very successful, reduced defect density, led major team effort, recognized leader, strong contributor, excellent results, develops employees, respected, proactive, team player, solves engineering problems	21.5	4
I1	5	3	6	6	4	5	4.8	Strong contributor, champions initiative, contributes & takes leadership role, mentors new members, strategic, superb communicator, recognizes & rewards performance, excellent team leader, utilizes available data, good company knowledge	22.5	1
M1	2	3	4	4	4	3	3.3	Successful, improved key processes, demonstrated consistent high results, made great strides in personal development, team player, good communication skills	19.7	22
P1	5	4	5	5	5	4	4.7	Implemented, installed, modified equipment, open to new ideas, active on teams, shares information, responsive to customer needs	20.4	20
S1	4	5	5	5	6	6	5.2	Outstanding manager, develops/promotes employees, lowest scrap, achieved stretch goals, heavy technical contributor, eliminates problems, highly cooperative, problem-solver, good team leader, effective communicator	22.7	2

First-Line Manager: Cumulative Systems, Performance Appraisal & Focal Rankings

1st-Line Manager	Bus. Strat	Belief	Bound	Diag	Inter. Act.	Align-ment	Avg.	Performance Appraisal Language	Ann. Achiev.	Focal Ranking
T1	4	3	5	4	5	4	4.2	Supported inventory adjustments, aggressive training, supported 'big picture' activities, carried engineering & management duties, strong leader, accomplished communicator	21.4	7
U1	4	5	5	5	5	5	4.8	Qualified & installed equipment, works well with others, respected by peers, regularly communicates, keen problem solving skills	20.0	14
V1	3	3	4	5	5	4	4.0	Successfully led shift, leader, strong team developer, effective communicator, problem-solver, responsive to customer needs	21.0	24
W1	5	6	6	6	5	5	5.5	Exceeds goals, developed employees, technical expert, led improvement efforts, good follow-through & communicator	20.7	5
X1	5	6	5	5	5	4	5.0	Yields hit new records, improved key processes, balanced & strong contributor, leader in change initiatives, team player, good communication skills, proactive, strong technical skills	22.6	10
Z1	3	3	4	4	4	3	3.5	Had good year, made improvements, reduced cycle time, increased activities, outstanding leadership & direction, works well with others	19.6	26
B2	4	3	5	5	5	4	4.3	Expert, key technology person, achieves goals, good leadership skills, organized, clear communicator, fast learner	21.7	2
D2	4	4	5	5	5	4	4.5	Met manufacturing indices, qualified & installed equipment, modified org. structure, strategic planner, good team developer & problem-solver	22	3
F2	5	4	5	5	4	3	4.3	Mature, well developed understanding of manufacturing & metrics, developing team, significant improvements, continuous improvement, team player, good problem-solving skills, responsive & reliable	21.1	11

First-Line Manager: Cumulative Systems, Performance Appraisal & Focal Rankings

1st-Line Mgr.	Bus. Strat	Belief	Bound	Diag	Inter Act.	Align- ment	Avg.	Performance Appraisal Language	Ann. Achiev	Focal Ranking
G2	4	4	5	5	5	3	4.3	Trained others, coordinated planning efforts, managed headcount, provided technical leadership, leads by example, facilitates teamwork & cooperation, technical leader	20.2	18
H2	4	3	5	4	4	4	3.8	Established training schedules, developed & qualified new technology, implemented measurement scale, team skills improving, very detail oriented, excellent follow-through	20	9
I2	5	6	6	6	5	5	5.5	Flexible, supported productivity improvement, managed critical processes, initiative, addresses strategic & tactical needs, strong technical skills, works well w/customers	19.2	15
J2	5	4	5	5	5	4	4.7	Exceeded goals, met training goals, building team, contributing member, good listener, team player	19.5	13
M2	4	4	5	5	5	4	4.5	Supportive of training, met indices, developing team, gets along well with others, communicates well	20	17
N2	3	3	4	5	5	3	3.8	Good contributor, strategic thinker, impressive improvement, contributed to module communications, supports customer needs, good production & technical skills	21.0	23
O2	2	4	5	6	5	5	4.5	Achieved most goals, lead team, reduced costs, supported engr efforts, trained staff, needs cross-functional leadership development, takes initiative, good follow-through	21.0	6
S2	5	4	4	5	5	4	4.5	Completed transition to new job, established staff training plans, achieved goals, completed multiple projects	18	21
T2	5	2	4	4	4	3	3.7	Sponsors & supports team, reactive, takes initiative, good working relationships with others, good problem-solver	19	25

Scatter Plots

Middle manager Scatterplot Matrix

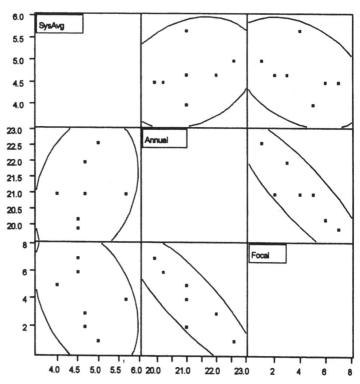

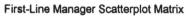

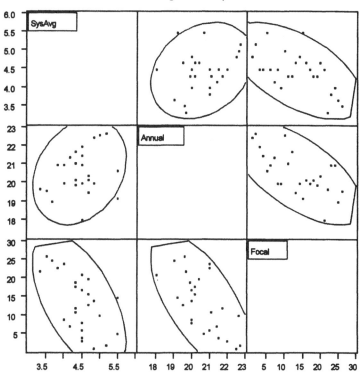

Glossary

Management Control System: The formal, information-based routines and procedures managers use to maintain or alter patterns in organizational activities. [Simons]

Business Strategy: A business strategy consists of the organization's plan (or course of action), pattern of action (or consistency of behavior), competitive position (or method of competing in a market) and overall perspective (shared frame of reference). [Adapted from Mintzberg]

Belief System: The explicit set of organizational definitions used to communicate formally and reinforce systematically the basic values, purpose and direction of the organization (credo's, mission statements, value statements, etc.). [Simons]

Boundary System: The formally stated rules and proscriptions by which the limits to opportunity-seeking behavior are established and communicated, based on business risks and strategy (policies, procedures, standards of conduct, etc.). [Simons]

Diagnostic Control System: The formal methods used by an organization to monitor progress towards organizational outcomes, goals, and correct for deviations from the standards set (profit plans, goals & objectives, project plans, strategic plans, etc.). [Simons]

Interactive Control System: The methods managers use to involve themselves regularly and personally in the decisions of subordinates in order to stimulate organizational learning, gain and share information, and focus attention on key strategic issues (meetings, strategic planing sessions, operational reviews, etc.). [Simons]

Manager: A person in a role in which he or she is held accountable not only for his/her personal effectiveness but also for the output of others; and is accountable for building and sustaining an effective team capable of producing those outputs. [Jaques]

First-Line Manager: A person in a role in which he or she is held accountable not only for his/her personal effectiveness but also for the output of individual contributors; and is accountable for building and sustaining an effective team of individual contributors capable of producing those outputs. [Adapted from Jaques]

Middle Manager: A person in a role in which he or she is held accountable not only for his/her personal effectiveness but also for the output of one or more first line managers; and is accountable for building and sustaining an effective team of first line managers capable of producing those outputs. [Adapted from Jaques]

Senior Manager: A person in a role in which he or she is held accountable not only for his/her personal effectiveness but also for the output of one or more middle managers; and is accountable for building and sustaining an effective team of middle managers capable of producing those outputs. [Adapted from Jaques]

Function: Main types of activity which follow from the objectives of the organization. [Jaques]

Role: The formal (job-related and explicit) and informal (social and implicit) part an individual plays in an organization or work group. [Moorhead & Griffin]

Task: An assignment to produce a specified output (including quality and quantity) within a targeted completion time, with allocated resources and methods and within specified limits (policies, procedures, rules, regulations, etc.) [Jaques]

Bibliography

Advanced Micro Devices. (1997). Neighbor to neighbor. (AMD Newsletter #90290). Austin, Texas.

Advanced Micro Devices. (1997). Neighbor to neighbor. (AMD Newsletter #90295). Austin, Texas.

Advanced Micro Devices. (1996). Neighbor to neighbor. (AMD Newsletter #90287). Austin, Texas.

Advanced Micro Devices. (1996). Annual Report. (AMD publication #90288). Sunnyvale, California.

Advanced Micro Devices. (1996). Purpose, vision, mission & values. (AMD brochure #90282). Austin, Texas.

Advanced Micro Devices. (1996). AMD at a glance. (AMD brochure #90238C). Sunnyvale, California.

Advanced Micro Devices. (1995). AMD corporate contributions guidelines & application. (AMD brochure #90249). Sunnyvale, California.

Advanced Micro Devices. (1995). Community involvement at AMD. (AMD brochure #90248). Sunnyvale, California.

Argyris, C. (1997). The next challenge. In M. Goldsmith and R. Beckhard (Eds.) The organization of the future. (pp. 367–374). San Francisco: Jossey-Bass.

Argyris, C. (1993). Knowledge for action: A guide to overcoming barriers to organizational change. San Francisco: Jossey-Bass.

Argyris, C. & Schön, D. (1974). Theory in practice: Increasing professional effectiveness. San Francisco: Jossey-Bass.

Barach, J. and Eckhardt, D. (1996). Leadership and the job of the executive. Connecticut: Quorum Books.

Barnard, C. (1938). The functions of the executive. Cambridge, Mass.: Harvard University Press.

Bennis, W. (1989). Why leaders can't lead: The unconscious conspiracy continues. San Francisco: Jossey-Bass.

Blackler F, and Shimmin, S. (1984). Applying psychology in organizations. London: Methuen.

Blalock, H. (1979). Social statistics. New York, McGraw Hill.

Block, P. (1993). Stewardship: Choosing service over self-interest. California: Berrett-Koehler.

Borg, W. R., & Gall, M. D. (1989). Educational research: An introduction. (5th Ed.). New York: Longman.

Bruning, J. & Kintz, B. (1997). Computational Handbook of Statistics. New York: Addison-Wesley Longman.

Campbell J. P. and Pritchard, R. D. (1976). Motivation theory in industrial and organizational psychology. Handbook of
Industrial and Organizational Psychology. Chicago, Rand-McNally.

Champy, James. (1995). Reengineering management: The mandate for new leadership. New York: Harper Business. p. 129–148.

Child, J. (1969). British management thought. London: Allen & Unwin.

Clark, J. V. (1960). Motivation in work groups: A tentative view.Human Organization. V13. pp. 199–208.

Clemmer, Jim. (1991). Firing on all cylinders: The service/quality system for high powered corporate performance. Toronto: Macmillan of Canada.

Coleman, J.S. (1990). Foundations of social theory. Massachusettes: Harvard University Press.

Collins, J. & Porras, J. (1994). Built to last: Successful habits of visionary companies. New York: HarperCollins Publishers.

Covey, Stephen R. (1989). The seven habits of highly effective people: Powerful lessons in personal change. NY: Simon & Schuster.

Deming, E. W. (1986). Out of the crisis. Massachusetts Institute of Technology, Center for Advanced Engineering Study: Cambridge, Mass. p. 23.

Denzin, N. K. & Lincoln, Y.S. (1994). Handbook of qualitative research. Thousand Oaks, CA: Sage.

Drucker, P. (1954). The practice of management. New York: Harper & Row.

Evans, M. G. (1970).The effects of supervisory behavior on the path goal relationships. Organizational Behavior and Human Performance. Vol. 5. pp. 277–298.

Fayol, H. (1930). General and industrial Management. London: Pitman & Sons.

Fincham, R. and Rhodes, P. S. (1988). The individual, work and organization. London: Weidenfeld & Nicolson.

Follet, M. O. (1941). Dynamic administration: The collected papers of Mary Parker Follet. Metcalf, H. C. (ed.) New York: Harper, 1941.

George, C. (1972). The history of management thought. New Jersey: Englewood Cliffs.

Goetz, J. P. & LeCompte, M.D. (1984). Ethnography and qualitative design in educational research. Oralando, FL: Academic Press.

Gordon, J. (Ed.). (1996). Industry Report : An Overview of Employee Training in America. Training, 33, 10.

Green, J. (Ed.). (1983). Worker's struggles: Past & Present. Penn: Temple University Press.

Guba, E. G., & Lincoln, Y. S. (1985). Effective evaluation. San Francisco: Jossey-Bass.

Gulick, L. & Urwick, L. (Eds.). (1937). Papers on the science of administration. New York: Institute of Public Administration.

Handy, C. (1989). The age of unreason. Boston: Harvard Business School Press.

Hanna, D.P. (1988). Designing organizations for high performance. New York: Addison-Wesley.

Herzberg, F., Mausner, B., Peterson, R. O., and Capwell, D. F. (1957). Job attitudes: Review of research and Opinion. Pittsburg: Psychological Service of Pittsburg.

House, R. J. (1971). A path-goal theory of leader effectiveness. In Current developments in the study of leadership, E. A. Fleishman & J. G. Hunt (eds.). Illinois, Southern Illinois University Press.

House, R. J. & Mitchell, T. R. (1974). Path-goal theory and leadership. Journal of Contemporary Business. Vol. 3., pp. 81–97.

Hoy, W. & Miskell, C. (1995). Educational administration: Theory, research & practice. New York: McGraw Hill.

Hubert, M. B. (1972). *Social Statistics*. New York: McGraw-Hill Book Company.

Huczynski, A. (1996). Management gurus: What makes them, and how to become one. Mass: Thompson Business Press.

Jaques, E. (1989). Requisite organization: The CEO's guide to creative structure and leadership. Virginia: Cason Hall & Co.

Kaplan, R. & Norton, D. (1996). The balanced scorecard: Translating strategy into action. Boston: Harvard Business School Press.

Karakekes, M., and Mc Daniel, G. L. (1996). Linking instructional design to organizational learning. In Designing Training Programs, Jack Phillips (Ed.). San Francisco: Jossey-Bass. pp. 289– 316.

Katz, D. & Kahn, R. L. (1966). The social psychology of organizations. New York: John Wiley.

Koontz, H. (1961). The management theory jungle. The Academy of Management Journal. December. pp. 174–188.

Kouzes, J. M., & Posner, B. Z. (1993). Credibility: How leaders gain and lose it, why people demand it. San Francisco: Jossey Bass.

Laird, D. (1985). Approaches to training & development., Revised, 2nd Ed. Mass: Addision Wesley.

Lorange, P. and Morton, M.S. (1974). A framework for management control. Sloan Management Review. Vol. 16. pp. 41–56.

Lupton, T. (1976). Best fit in the design of organizations, in Miller, E. J. (ed.). Task and Organization. New York: Wiley.

McCall, M. (1990). Whatever it takes: The realities of management decision making. New York: Simon & Schuster.

McClelland, D. (1973). Testing for competence rather than intelligence. American Psychologist, 28, 1–14.

Marshall, C., & Rossman, G. B. (1989). Designing qualitative research. Newbury Park: Sage.

Marsick, V. J. (1987). Learning in the workplace. London: Croom Helm.

Marsick, V. J., & Watkins, K. (1990). Informal and incidental learning in the workplace. NY: Routledge.

Maslow, A. H. (1943). A theory of human motivation. Psychological Review. 50:4. pp. 370–396.

Matheson, M. T. (1974). Some reported thoughts on significant management literature. Academy of Management Journal. Vol. 17. pp. 386–389.

Merchant, K. (1985). Control in business organizations. Mass: Pitman.

Merriam, S. (1984). Selected writings on philosophy and adult education. Florida: Krieger.

Mink, O. G., Owen, K.Q., & Mink, B.P. (1993). Developing high perfomance people: The art of coaching. Massachusettes: Addison-Wesley.

Mishler, E. G. (1986). Research interviewing: Context and narrative. Massachusettes: Havard University Press.

Moore, D.S. & McCabe, G. P. (1993). Introduction to the practice of Statistics. New York: W.H. Freeman & Company.

Moorhead, G. & Griffin, R. W. (1995). Organizational behavior: Managing people and organizations. New York: Houghton Mifflin.

Montana, P. J. & Charnov, B. H. (1993). Management, 2nd Ed. New York: Barron's Educational Series.

Morecroft J. & Sterman, J. (1994). Modeling for learning organizations. Portland: Productivity Press.

Murphy, E. (1996). Leadership IQ. New York: John Wiley & Sons.

Natemeyer, W. E. (ed.) (1978). Classics of organizational behavior. Illinois, Moore Publishing Co.

Newcomer, M. B. (1955). The big business executive: The factors that made him. New York.

Olian, J. D. & Rynes, S. L. (1992). Making total quality work: Aligning organizational processes, performance measures, and stakeholders. Human Resource Management, 30: 3.

Patton, M. Q. (1990). Qualitative evaluation and research methods. Newbury Park, Ca: Sage.

Phillips, J. (1991). Handbook of training and evaluation measurement methods. Texas : Gulf Publishing Co.

Potts. T. & Sykes, A. (1993). Executive talent: How to identify and develop the best. Illinois: Business One.

Quinn, R. E., Faerman, S. R., Thompson, M. P., McGrath, M. R. (1996). Becoming a master manager: A competency framework. N.Y: Joe Wiley & Sons.

Reinertsen, D. (1997) Managing the design factory. New York: Simon & Schuster.

Robers, E.M., and Gibson, D.V. (1991). Technology transfer and high technology industries. In D.V. Gibson (Ed.), Technology companies and global markets. Savage, MD: Rowman & Littlefield.

Robinson, D. G., & Robinson, J. C. (1989). Training for impact: How to link training to business needs and measure the results. San Francisco: Jossey Bass.

Rodengen, J. (1998). The spirit of AMD. Florida: Write Stuff Enterprises.

Sanders, W.J. (1997). Unleasing the power of the fifth wave. Remarks at the Networked Outlook Conference. (AMD publication 90281).

Sanders, W.J. (1996). An American crisis in education. Remarks at Femont Union High School District Foundation. (AMD publication 90289.)

Sanders, W.J. (1996). The best way to predict the future is to create it. Remarks to the 1996 Annual Shareholders' Meeting. (AMD publication 90279).

Sayles, Leonard R. (1993). The working leader: The triumph of high performance over conventional management principles. NY: The Free Press.

Schein, E. (1997). Leadership and organizational culture. In F. Hesselblein, M. Goldsmith & R. Beckhard (Eds.) The leader of the future. (pp. 59 - 70). San Francisco: Jossey-Bass.

Schön, D. (1987). Educating the reflective practitioner. San Francisco: Jossey-Bass.

Scott, W. R. (1981). Organizations: Rational, natural, and open systems. New Jersey: Prentice-Hall.

Senge, P. M. (1990). The fifth discipline: The art and practice of the learning organization. NY: Doubleday.

Senge, P. M. & Fulmer, R. M. Simulations, systems thinking and anticipatory learning. (1993). Journal of Management Development. 12:6, MCB Press.

Simon, H. (1957). Administrative behavior. New York: MacMillan.

Simon, H. (1997). Models of Bounded Rationality. Massachusets: The MIT Press.

Simons, R. (1990). The role of management control systems in creating competitive advantages: New perspectives. Accounting, Organizations and Society. London: Pergamon Press. 15:1/2. pp. 127–143.

Simons, R. (1994) How new top managers use control systems as levers of strategic renewal. Strategic Management Journal. Vol. 15. pp. 169–189.

Simons, R. (1995a). Levers of control: How managers use innovative control systems to drive strategic renewal. Harvard Business School Press, MA.

Simons, R. (1995b) Control in an age of empowerment. Harvard Business Review, March-April, p. 80–88.

Snedecor, G.W. & Cochran, W. G. (1989). Statistical Methods. Aimes: Iowa State University Press.

Spreitzer, G. M., & Quinn, R. E. (1996). Empowering middle managers to be transformational leaders. Journal of Applied Behavioral Science, 32, 237–261.

Stauss, A., & Corbin, J. (1990). Basics of qualitative research. Newbury Park: Sage.

Strake, R. (1996). Case Studies: In N.K. Denzin, Y.S., (Eds). Handbook of qualitative research. California: Sage.

Taylor, F. (1911). Principles of Scientific Management. New York: Harper.

Wagner, S.F. (1992). Introduction to Statistics. New York: HarperPerennial.

Weber, M. (1947). The theory of social and economic organizations. N.Y.: Free Press.

Wells, S. (1997). From sage to artisan: The nine roles of the value-driven leader. California: Davies-Black Publishing.

Yin, H . (1994). Case study research: Design & methods. California: Sage.

Zaleznik, A. (1997) Real work. Harvard Business Review. November–December. pp. 53– 63.

Index

Printed in the United States
by Baker & Taylor Publisher Services